Broken Walls

And Those Called to Repair Them

Kevin D. Kirkland

Table of Contents

Dedication

To my beautiful bride Kimberly, the mother of my children and my consummate helpmate in repairing the broken walls- This book would not exist without your love and support. Truth is, I would not truly exist without you. Your love overwhelms me, your encouragement carries me, and your walk with Jesus inspires me. I love you, no matter what.

To my children, Kaiden, Kait, and Kreed- I love you more than the words in a million books. Thank you for letting daddy spend all that time closed up in the office working on "the book." Remember that books will come and go, but the Word of the Lord endures forever. Love Jesus, worship Jesus, sing about Jesus, follow Jesus, and then teach those following you to do the same. I love you, no matter what.

To my father and mother- I could never say enough "thank you's" for the commitment you have made to train me and the girls to walk with Jesus. I recognize now the significance of the sacrifices you made to insure the spiritual walls around my life would be strong. I pray that you will get a glimpse of your spiritual legacy in these pages, but more than that, I pray my life will honor the overwhelming investment of love and support you have made in me. I hope one day my children can see me the way I see you. I love you, no matter what.

To my beautiful baby sisters- You have taught me much about what it means to lead, what it means to follow, and what it means to love. You have loved me even when I could never be all you dreamed that I was. Love your husbands passionately, rear your children in Jesus, and carry out the spiritual legacy that we have been given. I love you, no matter what.

To all of those who have gone before me on whose shoulders I stand to see the truth of God's Word and His commission to disciple the next generation- You are all to be honored more than I can offer in such few words. I pray that I will be for those following me, all you have been for me.

To Jesus- I love you. I love you. I love you.

April 16, 2007

Father, I know that you are aware of what happened today on the campus of Virginia Tech University. I have been watching the news coverage all day and listening to the response of our nation- my heart grieves for those who are suffering and for the young man that committed this horrible act. I cannot keep from believing that even though he is responsible for his actions, his actions are simply a result of those things that we have been planting in our young people from generation to generation- a result of our sin. I grieve because although some of those affected today are broken enough to cry out to you, so many will not. The psychobabble was instantaneous and continues from one "expert" to the next- my heart grows weary with the arrogance of our assumptions. We are people blinded to the spiritual reality of our own nation; our comfort and overwhelming selfishness have caused us to be void of repentance or humility.

I fear that just as we did after the hurricane in New Orleans and the events of 9/11, our arrogance will cause us to rally behind a pride-filled call to rebuild in our limited strength and we will refuse to turn and cry out to You. We have seemingly forgotten You, unless of course we need someone to blame. Deep in my soul, I also fear that even a tragedy of this evil nature will only awaken us long enough to hit the proverbial snooze button on our current reality until the next alarm sounds. Will the next alarm be the one that awakens us to The Truth? How long can we go on denying that we are in desperate need of something real, something powerful, something that can bring about true change? We need You oh, God.

Will we ever be able to see that events like today are works of the devil himself, and we are responsible for leaving the front door wide open? How long, oh God, until we see that the issues in our schools, our government, our prisons, our churches cannot be fixed by new legislation, better security, newer prescriptions, or better programming? Our homes are broken, our spiritual walls destroyed by our own complacency, our children are being raped and murdered by our own devices, and the men that you called to disciple the nations are too few and far between. So many of them have abandoned their Biblical responsibility to teach us, lead us, and stand on the wall in our spiritual defense.

Our pulpits are filled with lots of prosperity and positive thinking, and those who are willing to call out for repentance have lost their popularity. Can we change? Will this cry be just another voice in the wilderness, or can these words become a catalyst for true change, in our hearts, in our homes? I am ruined with these thoughts and far beyond the point of not putting pen to pad. Today, I am without the ability to go quietly into the night, so I will let the passion of this moment capture me, and I will put my trust and this pen in Your hand and ask that You compel me to speak with the fervor that consumes my soul. My heart is broken.

I repent of my own personal sin and the sin of my family-of our pride, our idolatry, our adultery, of taking Your Name to be used in vanity, of trusting the things our hands have made and of the complacency that has lulled us to sleep at the wheel of responsibility.

Our walls are broken and our gates are burned with fire-today we recognize our need for You, we respond in humility and brokenness, we repent, and we set our hearts on doing whatever it takes to truly rebuild our families, our homes, our nation. For Your Name's sake. For our children, and their children. . .

We need You King Jesus, nothing else will do.

My pen, your hand,
Kevin

As the Lord lives, what the Lord says to me, that I will speak. 1 Kings 22:14

Introduction

I just want to say a couple of things as an introduction. The note that you have just read was a journal entry I made to the Lord the day of the Virginia Tech shootings. It was on that day, I relented to the Lord to write this book. I included it because I wanted to remind myself of the fervor of the moment in which I wrote it to Him. This book is truly my heart's cry, and I penned it with an incredible amount of love in my heart for my Jesus, the young people of Generation Next, and for you. There will be some moments of true candor and emotion in our time together, but I want you to know that it is with great personal conviction and a true heart to honor the revelations of the Lord, that I have included these things. For the past five years, this book was forged on napkins, sticky notes or whatever else was at hand when God moved in my spirit; but more importantly, God has been writing it on my heart. The backdrop for so much of God's penmanship has been my own personal arrogance and fallacies, so please bear with me as I seek to honor only Him through this book.

Having said that, let me make it clear that I am not an expert of any kind, and this is not a "how to" book on parenting. I suppose it is more of a "why to" book on spiritual parenting. It is a cry for the people of God to take up the mantle of discipleship for the lost and broken children of the coming generations in our country. I have included some practical things that will no doubt be of use in parenting, but most of the tools that we will discuss for restoration are simply about the call of God on our lives to come to Him in our brokenness. I pray that through our time together, your heart will be convicted, encouraged, and consumed by the love of the God we serve and the call He has given each of us. I pray that as God reveals Himself to us, my heart and your heart would be connected by one common purpose-that each of us would commit to becoming a:

Repairer of the Broken Walls

The Blueprint
For the past decade, I have spent almost every waking moment of my life with the young people of America. Like many of you who serve children or students in some capacity, I have cried myself to sleep many nights with the burdens and brokenness of the next generation on my mind. I have petitioned the Lord for years on end for direction and wisdom regarding how to go about seeing the next generation rescued. Like lots of folks, I could point to the problems, but I was void of a solution that could bring about lasting change. I tried every kind of youth program I could get my hands on. I read books by "experts" on young people. I went to conferences and studied culture until I was blue in the face. I was "purpose-driven" and cutting edge, but the walls just kept coming down. Children and young people alike were still struggling to survive. Homes were still breaking apart in record numbers. Teenagers were still killing themselves and their classmates, and they were still less and less interested in the "church."

Then, about four years ago, God began to paint a picture for me through a young man in His Word named Nehemiah.

This incredible picture of restoration was there all along- in His Word, just like He said it would be. God was calling me back to the basics- back to Him. The story came alive to me, and God began to show me piece by piece the process that He designed for us to follow in restoring the spiritual walls upon which our children are reliant. I fell in love with Nehemiah- with the brokenness he feels for the people of God and the name of God, with the humility he exhibits in repentance, and with the passion and courage that drive him to be the catalyst for one of the greatest moves of restoration in history. There it was- the blueprint for rebuilding. Nehemiah gives us the perfect process for revival, restoration, and rebuilding- a process that together we must begin today.

This is a not a book about programs, cultural trends, or cutting edge ministry methods; this is a book about Jesus, about the devastation of sin and the restoration of repentance. Unlike so many of the solutions we have devised to put a stop to the death and destruction of today's children and young people, the restoration process of Nehemiah is contingent not upon what we can do, but upon what has already been done for us by Jesus. This process is not only the perfect process for the restoration of the souls of those following us, it is the exact process that you and I must learn to live out in our everyday lives if we desire restoration in our own souls.

In the following pages, we are going to be discussing the pieces of this process in detail. The similarities of the devastation in Nehemiah's time and the brokenness of today's America will be at the forefront of our conversation. More importantly, the steps that Nehemiah follows for the restoration of his nation are the very keys that I believe God has called us to utilize in the rebuilding of that which the enemy has destroyed in our own land. As a backdrop, I want to give you a brief summary of Nehemiah's story. I have included the scriptures from much of Nehemiah chapters one and two, but I would encourage you to take a minute at the end of this introduction to read the first few chapters of the book of Nehemiah to familiarize yourself with his entire story. Just hang in there with me for a few pages so that we can develop a solid foundation for the rest of our conversation. Let me set up the story for you:

Nehemiah is a Jewish exile who has risen to a high office in the Persian Empire. He is a cupbearer to the king named Artaxerxes. He is not a royal butler as some would assume; he is more like a personal advisor to the emperor of the world. After Nehemiah's country, Israel, is destroyed by King Nebuchadnezzar, Nehemiah finds himself living in the capital of the Persian Empire, Susa. Today, Susa is called Shush and sits about 150 miles from the Persian Gulf in Iran. As you may already know, after years of disobedience, idol worship, and pagan ways, God uses King Nebuchadnezzar and the Babylonians to destroy the nation of Israel and the city of Jerusalem. An untold number of people die from the war, the pestilence, and of starvation- the rest of the Jews are taken into captivity by the Babylonians, which is how Nehemiah finds himself in Susa. The nation of Israel, the Jews, God's chosen people, are scattered from one end of the world to the other, but as foretold by the prophet, Jeremiah, after seventy years in captivity, God begins to bring His people back to Jerusalem and back to Him. Nehemiah is living in a time for rebuilding. So are we.

The Process Begins. . .

Recognize

Circa 445 B.C., 140 years after the destruction of the city of Jerusalem and the temple of God, Nehemiah gets a wake-up call that puts into motion the process of rebuilding.

*The words of Nehemiah son of Hacaliah: In the
month of Kislev in the twentieth year, while I was
in the citadel of Susa, Hanani, one of my brothers,
came from Judah with some other men, and I ques-
tioned them about the Jewish remnant that survived
the exile, and also about Jerusalem. They said to me,
"Those who survived the exile and are back in the
province are in great trouble and disgrace. **The wall
of Jerusalem is broken down, and its gates have
been burned with fire.**" Nehemiah 1:1-3*

Although a fellow named Ezra was already welcoming
Jews back to Jerusalem and working on rebuilding the
temple of God, Nehemiah's brother, Hanani, tells him that
the situation there is desperate. Hanani relays the horrible
news that the city gates are burned with fire and the city
walls have been broken down. Now, you have to understand
that in those days, the city walls and their gates were the only
source of protection the people had from their enemies- they
did not have fighter jets and smart bombs. The broken walls
make the children of God and the city of God vulnerable to
the attacks of any and every enemy. Although Nehemiah is
incredibly concerned about the physical brokenness of the
city of God, his heart is truly undone by the spiritual brokenness of the nation of Israel, his nation- the people of God.
Nehemiah knows something must change.

It is important to remember that Jerusalem is not just
any city- it is the city of God. Jerusalem is the very place
where God chose to build His temple- His place of residence and worship on the Earth. The welfare of the city, its
walls, and God's temple are of incredible spiritual significance. Jerusalem's physical brokenness is a picture of the
spiritual brokenness of God's children. Their devastation is
in contrast to the great and awesome God they represent.
Nehemiah understands all of this. He sees the situation for

the emergency that it truly is, and he takes the first step to rebuilding the city of Jerusalem, to rebuilding the people of God. **Nehemiah recognizes that the people of God, the city of God, are desperate for something to change. This is exactly where you and I must start our rebuilding effort- by recognizing we are in need of one.**

Responsibility

Not only does Nehemiah recognize the brokenness of the people of God, he is also well aware of how their devastation came about. He sees clearly his responsibility in the process of rebuilding the city of Jerusalem and to the coming generations of the nation of Israel. This will be one of the most important parts of our discussion as we look closely at God's commission for each of us and His expectations about our responsibility to the next generation.

Respond

Upon hearing of the devastation in Jerusalem, Nehemiah responds in the most incredible way. He responds according to the very heart of God.

> *When I heard these things, I sat down and wept. For some days I mourned and fasted and prayed before the God of Heaven. Nehemiah 1:4*

As soon as he acknowledges the truth about the disgrace of God's city and the devastation of God's people, Nehemiah is broken to the point of weeping, mourning, and fasting for days. He responds out of the heart of God with brokenness, conviction, passion, and inspiration. His brokenness pushes him beyond the comfort of the Persian Empire, and his actions are a beautiful example of exactly how we should respond to the devastation that surrounds us.

Remember God

> *Then I said: "O LORD, God of Heaven, the great and awesome God, who keeps his covenant of love with those who love Him and obey His commands, let your ear be attentive and your eyes open to hear the prayer your servant is praying before you day and night for your servants, the people of Israel. Nehemiah 1:4-6*

Nehemiah remembers the promise of God to rebuild the people, to rebuild the city, and he knows that God is the only source for the healing they need. He remembers that the God of the universe is the great and awesome God, and he declares that he and the people of Israel are completely dependent upon Him for restoration. Like Nehemiah, we too must remember the great and awesome God and put away our dependence on mere man and the fallible wisdom of the world.

Repentance

> **I confess the sins we Israelites, including myself and my father's house, have committed against you. We have acted very wickedly toward you. We have not obeyed the commands, decrees and laws you gave your servant Moses.** *Remember the instruction you gave your servant Moses, saying, "If you are unfaithful, I will scatter you among the nations, but if you return to me and obey my commands, then even if your exiled people are at the farthest horizon, I will gather them from there and bring them to the place I have chosen as a dwelling for my Name." Nehemiah 1:6-9*

Nehemiah understands that the sins of the people of God and their arrogance are the reason for their brokenness, and he is willing to repent of not only his personal sin, but the sins of the generations before him. Nehemiah's humility and honesty before the Lord is the catalyst that puts into motion a move of God unlike anything previously recorded. Sin is the reason for the devastation in our land, and we must repent in humility and brokenness if we desire to see true change.

Risk

The king said to me, "What is it you want?" Then I prayed to the God of Heaven, and I answered the king, "If it pleases the king and if your servant has found favor in his sight, let him send me to the city in Judah where my fathers are buried so that I can rebuild it." Nehemiah 2:4-5

After four months of prayer, Nehemiah puts his life on the line to start the rebuilding process. By going before the king, Nehemiah takes a risk- he takes a step of faith, quits his job, and answers the call of God on his life. He is not waiting around for someone else to complete the task; he sets his heart on rebuilding the city and the people of God and surrenders his life to its completion. It could have cost him everything including his life, but he is abandoned to this purpose and cannot simply go quietly into the night while the next generation of God's people suffers and while the name of God is defamed.

Rebuilding Tools

In chapters two and three of the book of Nehemiah, we see the actual rebuilding begin to take shape. There are several things about this process that you and I must learn in order to be effective re-builders of the spiritual walls in our society.

Nehemiah faces trouble on every side. There are continued attacks and uprisings against the walls being rebuilt and the gates being reestablished. We will spend quite a bit of time discussing the tools for our rebuilding during this section including some very powerful and practical ways to reach the next generation. I want to challenge you with some simple concepts that can be established both through our homes and our churches that will help us practically live out the call of God on our lives to rebuild.

Reward

> *So the wall was completed on the twenty-fifth of Elul, in fifty-two days. When all our enemies heard about this, all the surrounding nations were afraid and lost their self-confidence, because they realized that this work had been done with the help of our God. Nehemiah 6:15-16*

Fifty-two days. . . Nehemiah and the Jews completed the rebuilding of the city walls in just fifty-two days! Even by modern standards, this would be considered a miraculous move of God. Nehemiah honors God in humility, honesty, and by making himself available for the task of rebuilding. God answers his fervent prayer by supernaturally interceding on behalf of His people. God rebuilds the city in such a way that no man could take the credit. We need this kind of supernatural intercession by a Holy God today in our homes, our churches, our cities, and our schools. As God honors the process of brokenness, humility, repentance, and availability in Nehemiah, He will honor our hearts to rebuild as well. The blueprint for rebuilding is in place; all we need now are the repairers of the broken walls.

Are you ready?

Section One

Spiritual Orphas

Chapter One

Wake Up

Three a.m. I could hear the sound of my cell phone vibrating on my dresser. It was not just vibrating, it was blaring that awful ring tone that sounds when I get a text message. It is a hard sound to describe and awful enough during the day, but at three in the morning, it is beyond annoying. I got up with every intention of throwing the phone out the window, before I realized that it was a message from one of our missionaries in Kenya. Our ministry had only been in Kenya for a month, and we had two twenty-two year-old young ladies living there in an orphanage they were helping manage. There is an eight hour time difference between the States and Kenya, so I knew it must have been something serious for the girls to send it to me in the middle of the night. The message stated, "Orpha is very sick, please pray." I knew who Orpha was because the girls had relayed to me that one of the children in the orphanage was showing some signs of illness. I, however, was in no way prepared for my next correspondence with them. I received the following email from Julie and Kim at 7:55 a.m. on Tuesday, July 15th, 2005.

Yesterday, we had to rush Orpha to the emergency room in town (45 minutes away) because she had been vomiting all night and most of the time it was full of blood. She was not in control of her body and she was obviously dehydrated. Before we left she began to get cold in her feet, and I knew right away from this that we needed to go quickly. As I was driving and Kim was trying to hold Orpha in the seat next to me, I kept praying that the Lord would heal her. I know that He is more than capable, so I prayed it believing completely. At the same time, I had this feeling that all of this was the Lord preparing me for the bad news to come. We arrived at the hospital, and it was obvious that we were not in America anymore. They really didn't care that she was dying and took their time. They took her temperature and said it was 65 F, I did not know that was possible. They put an IV in but it would not pump because she was so dehydrated, but more so because all the doctors were at the opening of a new building and the people in charge had no idea what they were doing. I basically had to do the IV for them. Anyway, her condition was bad. After two hours or so they admitted her with hopes that the doctor would come and see her that evening. In the wards here, there are beds just shoved next to each other so only one person is allowed to stay. The matron stayed with Orpha because she can communicate better. When we left Orpha kept saying, "Don't leave me here," and it broke my heart to leave, but we had no choice.

We arrived this morning to find out that one and a half hours after we left, she passed away. She began to experience more and more pain in her legs and the doctor did not see her. She told the matron, "Why did Julie and Kim leave me here to die, I want to go home." The matron said that right before she died she said, "I am ready to go now, tell everyone its okay," and passed away. On the way here yesterday, we asked her all the questions to make sure that she knew the Lord, there was no doubt, and even in all the pain she smiled and said, "Yes."

I would like to sound spiritual and say that I understand it all, but I don't. I know that the Lord is good no matter what, and I trust Him completely and love Him a little more today than yesterday. I know that it is going to be by His strength that I make it through going home today to tell her brother, Dennis, and the other 40 children who are expecting her back today.

There are so many things that are hard to deal with. . . I have experienced death so many times with people who were very close to me, but this is so different from all of those things. She was twelve years old, a child, who could not help the disease that she had, nor the fact that no one would get her treatment. She was truly helpless in this situation. I know that she is in a better place where she is not experiencing pain or sorrow or the tears that have been in her eyes for the past couple of days. I see how death is just something you deal with, but don't show to others, that she had HIV and it was expected, that she is an orphan so it really doesn't matter, and in the mortuary when I went to see her body, I never in my wildest imagination thought I would be walking into a room stacked with bodies and have them pull her body out on the same table as a man who had been shot in the head, and in a freezer with about 50 other bodies. I was thinking there would be closure in this, but really it just made the reality that to them she is just another victim of HIV more evident.

I think I have talked enough. I hope that I have not provided too much detail, but it helps to get some of this out. I know that you are concerned and care, and I thank you for your love and prayers. Please continue to pray for this place, I wish I could explain it all. The Lord is still Good, He still provides, protects, loves, guides, and saves. I love you all very much.

No matter what,
Julie

Orpha had HIV/AIDS because a relative raped her before she came to the orphanage. At the time of her death, she also had tuberculosis, worms, and syphilis. Julie and Kim held a funeral service for her. They bought a coffin from a street vendor on the side of the road and buried her not too far from the orphanage on one of the most beautiful pieces of land you have ever seen. Orpha was an orphan; she had a beautiful smile and a captivating personality; she loved to dance and sing. Her soul belonged to Jesus, but her physical body died at only twelve years old because those called to protect her did not, those called to love her were gone, and those called to care for her selfishly abused her. Many orphans have died in this village and continue to today, but this was the first funeral for an orphan that they have ever seen. Orpha may have lived for at least a little while longer had the doctors not been too busy opening a new building; she may have lived much longer had the adults in her life recognized that she was sick and cared enough to do something about it. Orpah's death was not the result of her own actions. She was an orphaned child, and in Africa orphaned children die everyday. I am really without words to explain the emotions I feel just penning this story. An estimated 22,000,000 adults and children were living with HIV in Sub-Saharan Africa at the end of 2007. In 2007 alone, 1.5 million Africans died from AIDS leaving behind 11.6 million orphans[1]. This is the reality of Africa. It is not a story in a book you can open and close- it is an alarm. I am awake forever for Orpha.

At one time or another, all of us experience a "wake up" call like this one. The phone call in the middle of night that you know is the news about a death or tragedy of someone close to you; the moment your teenage daughter comes in and sits down at the kitchen table and tells you that she is pregnant; standing in the doctor's office with your wife of twenty years as the doctor comes in with the news that you have cancer, or even the moment when your son or daughter is born. Moments captured in time like a photograph- moments that cause the Earth under us to move; moments that shake everything in our lives that can be shaken. These moments do not leave you. They do not allow you to just move on; even the details of the moment are forever trapped in your mind by your senses. You can remember the smell of the doctor's office or the exact path your daughter's tears took as they rolled off her face.

Each of us has experienced these moments individually, but as a nation, it seems we have experienced them time and again. I remember the events of 9/11 like they were yesterday- I think most of us can remember exactly where we were and what we were doing when we heard the news. Millions of us stood frozen as we watched the reality of our nation change before our eyes as the twin towers fell and crushed downtown New York. In this moment, we knew America would never be the same. We remember the images of bloody teenagers running for their lives out of Columbine High School, and the vile nature of the video diaries the gunman from the Virginia Tech shootings left us.

It is these "wake up" calls that interrupt us; they remind us of the reality of the world we live in, and they change our perspectives, our priorities. They cause us to take a deep look at how and why we live our lives, how we spend our time, our energy, and our resources. These moments define who our true friends are, and they push us to examine relationships with our spouses and our children. They make the world seem simple again; they bring the craziness of life to a halt- they make the big things seem small and the small things important all over. They make the words, "I love you," mean something once again. They cause us to question everything- they wake us up often times from a dead sleep. In a strange way we need them; though we seldom welcome them, it is the alarms of life that keep us from being asleep at the wheel. It is these moments that provide clarity and vision, that purify our heart's desires, that take us to our wits end- they bring sight to the blind and inspiration to the complacent; they wreck us and heal us all at the same time.

My hope is that today will be such a moment. My heart pounds out of my chest to sound an alarm that will forever wake us up. It is not about one single tragedy; for most of us, is it related to them all. It is about our children and their children- about the generation of young people in our own country who are spiritual Orphas. The travesties of Africa are well documented and overt, but it is the spiritual Orphas of America who fill the halls of our schools and the streets of our cities seemingly without a voice.

The truth is that what is happening in Africa physically has been happening spiritually in America for a long time. Our children are being spiritually abused, orphaned, and left to die in a culture where those called to protect them have not, those called to love them are missing, and those called to teach them the things of God have failed them.

This is not a book you can open and close; this is the reality of America. I want to dig deep into this reality and allow God to spur us on to changing it. My prayer is that the revelations of this book will be not only an alarm that wakes us to the truth of where we are as a people, but that you and I will learn how to respond to that truth in a way that honors God and moves us to start the process of rebuilding our homes, our families, our children, our churches, our schools, and our cities. In the deepest part of who I am, I believe that God is sounding the alarm, that He is calling us to awaken fathers, mothers, teachers, coaches, pastors- to awaken an entire generation of adults to the cries of our children, and our children's children.

I want you to join me on this journey of personal revival, repentance, restoration, and rebuilding. I need you to join me on this journey of revival for our children and their children. If you cannot see that we are in need of one, you should definitely read on.

> ***Wake up!*** *Strengthen what remains and is about to die, for I have not found your deeds complete in the sight of my God. Remember, therefore, what you have received and heard; obey it, and repent. But if you do not wake up, I will come like a thief, and you will not know at what time I will come to you. Revelation 3:2-3*

Section Two

Recognize

Chapter Two

We Are Lost

It is one of the most prominent principals in the Bible; in all of life.

You will never be rescued until you first recognize that you are lost.

My name is Kevin D. Kirkland, and I am a sinner in need of a savior. Our admittance that we are broken and lost is the key to our salvation- to our revival, to our rebuilding effort. This is where we start, by recognizing that the spiritual state of our children is broken. We start by recognizing that the spiritual walls surrounding the coming generations in America are broken down, and the gates into their lives are burned with fire.

The process begins. Remember Nehemiah? He is not living in the broken down slums of Jerusalem; he was living in the comfort of the Persian palace. His eyes are not opened to the devastation of the people of God until the day his brother brings him the horrible news about the situation in Jerusalem. For the first time, Nehemiah recognizes the truth of the brokenness existing in the people of God.

The city of Jerusalem existed in peril for over 100 years. The people of God were captives to the nation of Babylon since before Nehemiah was born. The spiritual brokenness of the Jews is surely not news to Nehemiah but upon hearing the details of the devastation in Jerusalem, something awakes him to the truth. Much of what we are about to expose is not news to us, but we must choose to wake up to the truth. This is the beginning of the rebuilding process, but getting started is always hard to do especially when it comes to admitting our own brokenness.

The American Disadvantage

I traveled to Africa many times before Orpha's death and saw the pestilence with my own eyes, but I was asleep to the reality of the real issues that face their continent until that early morning text message. As obvious as the issues of Africa are, still I slept. I did not start helping rebuild Africa until the day I woke up to the truth. Here is the problem: We live in America. We are not physically dying in record numbers, we are not overcome by disease, or pestilence; our walls are strong, our military the best in the world, our economy lives on, and our medical expertise is unrivaled. Our advantages have become our greatest disadvantage.

In Africa, you cannot help but see the death and destruction the devil has brought to their land, but in America everything has a nice ribbon and bow attached to it. The disintegration of the spiritual fibers of our nation is no less obvious, but the enemy has subtlety lulled us to sleep. We are blinded by our own selfishness and the overall comfort of life in America. And while the awareness of the physical pestilence and disease here and abroad has been raised over the last decade, when it comes to the spirituality of the next generation, no one is raising the red flag. The truth remains hidden under our fancy churches with their tall steeples and million-dollar fountains; the state of our union is summed up in a two hour political spin once a year, and we are spiritually sleepwalking through the alarms sounding daily from the front page of our newspapers. Like those called to care for my friend Orpha, we are opening new buildings while our children fight for their spiritual lives.

No, there are not 22,000,000 people in our country infected with a deadly disease, but according to the Alan Guttmacher Institute we have brutally aborted (murdered) more than 45,000,000 innocent babies in this country from 1973 to 2005 (That number does not include those in the past three years[2]. Adolph Hitler, considered one of the most evil men to ever live, was credited with killing 11 million people). Millions of children are not living in the streets of America, but even here in one of the wealthiest nations on the planet, there are almost 37,000,000 people living below the poverty line; 13,000,000 of whom are children under the age of 18[3]. Although the U.S. government spends around $175,000,000 a year on abstinence-based programs designed to slow the sexual activity of teenagers, a reported 70% of young people have engaged in sexual intercourse by the time they are nineteen years old[4]. In 2005, 37% of the 4,100,000 children born in the United States were born to unmarried women. That is 1.5 million children[5].

No, there are not 11,000,000 children in our country physically orphaned by HIV, but there are countless millions of children being spiritually orphaned everyday by divorce, the consumption of the corporate world, and the lack of spiritual discipline from those charged with rearing them in The Truth. We do not see millions of children dying in our country of starvation, but there are millions spiritually starving to death every Sunday in churches where the Bread of Life has been traded in for the "self-help" gospel. All of these truths and still we sleep. **Our freedom has destroyed our ability to see that we are slaves to our own devices.** This is our disadvantage- we are lost and broken but refuse to recognize the severity of our spiritual devastation. We will never be rescued until we first recognize that we are lost.

The Snooze Button

According to Christian researcher George Barna, there are currently 100,000,000 un-churched people in America (more than 25% of which are ages 0-17). If the un-churched of America made up their own country, it would be the 12th largest country in the world[6]. With the advancement of each generation, the percentages of the un-churched continue to increase. While we build more and more church buildings and tout the success of our mega churches, fewer and fewer of our children truly know how to walk with Jesus. I could inundate you with statistic after statistic about the spiritual epidemics in our country, but the numbers cannot begin to tell the whole truth.

Something is amiss in our nation. Something is terribly wrong in our children, and each time another Columbine or Virginia Tech wakes us up to evil that has penetrated the hearts of our children, it seems like we are only awake long enough to hit the proverbial snooze button. With each passing display of the ugly truth that lies just beneath the surface, we turn to the latest psychobabble to convince ourselves it will not happen again- until it happens again. I hope we are far enough down the road to recognize that these alarms will keep sounding, and truthfully, unless something changes in the hearts of the next generation, these events are simply the preamble to something worse.

> "Today's tragedy becomes the event that plants the seed for tomorrow's crisis.[7]"
>
> -Ronald Stephen, National
> School Safety Center

There have been over 229 violent deaths in American schools since the attack on Columbine in April of 1999.[8] In all honesty, the only event I can truly recall hearing about was the massacre on the campus of Virginia Tech. I hate to harp on the school violence trend, but these things keep happening and we keep ignoring the obvious- something must change. Let me ask you a question. When was the last time you thought about the tragedy that happened at Virginia Tech before reading the first page of this book? Unless you were directly involved, the answer is probably troubling. I do not want to be "that guy" continually declaring "the sky is falling," but as a people, we move on too fast. We are awake for a moment and our hearts are stirred to change, but before we can truly commit ourselves to the process of rebuilding, we are comfortably sleeping again, and the sky is still falling.

The people of Israel in the days of the Old Testament are plagued with this exact problem. God sounds the alarm and for a moment they are awakened to their reality without Him; unfortunately, soon after they find themselves dead asleep once again. God sends judge after judge to rouse them to the reality of their SIN problem and prophet after prophet warns them of the coming judgment, but they never seemed to stay awake long enough to avoid destruction. Time and again, God opens the door for us to acknowledge our SIN problem, but nothing has changed in us. We simply figure out a way to cope with the pain of the moment until the next tragedy happens. Rather than sound the alarm and rally the troops, we just prop ourselves up in our own arrogance and limp on as if we are not broken at all, denying ourselves the true healing that God desires to bring us. This is not a cry for more security cameras or better law enforcement; these issues are only the outward signs of the inward issues- spiritual issues- SIN issues.

In my home office, I have a small mantle on the wall above the computer that I am typing on right now with several pictures of my children, a really great picture of my wife and I kissing (Hi babe- love ya bunches), my ordination certificate into the gospel ministry, a gourd from a village leader in a small village in Kenya (long story), a small Bible that belonged to a soldier in World War II, and a black and white picture of rows and rows of freshly covered graves I took in South Africa. When I first began getting the mantle in order, my wife came in and "oohed" and "awed" over the sweet pictures of the children and the picture of us, but when she got to the picture of the graves she said, "Kevin, that is horrible and morbid. Why would you put that right there in front of you everyday?" I did not have to think about my response, "Because it reminds me of the reality that is our world and on those days when I am asleep at the wheel, it awakens me to the truth. Then, I remember our desperate need for a Savior." Death is certain, hell is forever, and it is filling up fast. I am awake again, and there is no time left for subtleties.

Chapter 3

The Greeter Guy

Some of you are thinking to yourself, "Well things are not that bad, and this guy is just a little over the top." Don't worry, you are not the first to look at me like that- the problem is I know better. I know that by simply opening our eyes we can see clearly that things are amiss- so often it is not that we do not see clearly, it is our unwillingness to admit the devastation that has plagued us, especially those of us in the Church. For so long when asked how things are in our city, we have effortlessly replied, "Oh they are great, our church is doing great and we love our pastor, and the kids programs are good, etc." It is our trained, politically correct response, and while it may be true for the little "holy huddle" so many of us live in, the overall truth of our city is just like the overall truth of every city- broken.

Every week we get up on Sunday, dress up real nice for Jesus, and then we put on the "face." The doors swing open and there is that guy. You know the guy that has the plastered on smile standing at the door with a program of how we are going to worship God today with a name tag identifying him as a "greeter." He is the one who asks us that timeless question, "Well, how are you today?" Like Pavlov's dogs, we respond without even thinking, "I'm fine." You knew it didn't you- you knew what I was going to say, and for some of us on some Sundays that is the truth, we are "fine," but for an overwhelming majority of our country, "fine" is a big fat lie.

Let me illustrate the reality of this issue with a story from my own childhood. On the way to church one Sunday morning, my sister and I were in the back of the suburban fighting. (I was winning.) Even though she is three years younger, I was beating her up pretty good. That was back in the days when seat belts did not exist in the back seats of cars. We had all the seats down so we could move around- it was like a moving jungle gym. My mom was yelling at us from the front seat, "If you kids don't stop fighting, I am going to wear you out." That was also back in the days when you could spank your children with branches off trees and nobody thought anything about it. By the time we arrived at church, mom had had it "up to here."

When we got out in the church parking lot, there was not a soul in sight, really bad news for me. My mom proceeded to spank me all the way to the front door. She was doing that "syllable and swat" method- you know where she was dragging me with one hand and was spanking me with the other. With incredible symmetry there was a swat perfectly timed in sequence with every syllable of every word. "I (swat) TOLD (swat) YOU (swat) TO (swat) STRAIGHTEN UP (swat, swat. . . swat.)" And then it happened, the front doors of the church flew open, and there he was, "Greeter Guy." Sure enough here it came, "Wellll Kirkland Family, how are you today?" I saw my very first miracle right there. In the twinkling of an eye, my mom transformed from a fire-breathing dragon into a graceful swan, and without even a pause to breathe she answered, "We're fine." I wanted to shout, "She is lying; she is trying to kill me, call someone! Don't just stand there and greet, I am in trouble here! We are not fine, that is not the truth!"

I will never forget that day. My mother was right to discipline me, but watching her transform that day is what truly settled in my memory. Later on, when I regained consciousness, I remember thinking, "Why do we have to be fine? Is it wrong to have some issues and be in church or something?" Think about it. We have all experienced this at one time or another. Here is what I want you to do next Sunday when the "greeter guy" ask you how you are: Tell him the truth! The truth might be that you are great so share with him why you are great, but that may not be the truth at all. When he asks you, just tell him, "Welllll, since you asked. I am struggling with an old addiction to pornography again; I am working way too much; I feel disconnected from my wife and children; my mother has breast cancer, and I have not read my Bible in six months." He probably will not be standing there when you get there next week. When he sees you coming, he will remember some other "greeter" chores that he forgot to do. I have nothing against the "greeter guy," I have been him on many occasions, but can you see how quickly we learn to put aside the truth of our reality just to keep from having to deal with it? We are sleep-walking from one day to the next like little children playing "hide and seek." They cover their eyes and think if they cannot see you, then you do not exist.

What if Nehemiah's brother had responded that way when Nehemiah asked about Jerusalem? "Welllll, brother, things in Jerusalem are hunky dory. Everything is just fine." No. When Nehemiah asked his brother about the condition of the city, of the people, his brother recognized the truth. He could have said, "Well Ezra and the finance committee have really got a good "temple" building program. The pledges are rolling in, and I really like the color they chose for the angels by the altar." Come on- just because we do not want it to be true, does not make it less true. This is not about being pessimistic or negative, but it is past time that we open our eyes to the spiritual condition of our land. We need some people to be over the top; people who are not afraid to shout the alarm from the rooftop. The prophets of Israel were over the top, and if the people of Israel would have recognized the truth about the spiritual state of their country, then Jerusalem would not have been destroyed to start with or been enslaved to other nations.

The Great Cover-Up

Let me give you a Biblical picture of exactly how all this "covering-up" started so we can figure out how to move beyond it. As soon as sin enters the picture in Genesis chapter two, brokenness, shame, and fear come with it. This is the beginning of the "great cover-up." Adam and Eve know they sinned, and they recognize instantly that they feel ashamed for the first time, so they do what we have been doing ever since then, they cover up. Genesis 2:25 tells us that before sinning, Adam and Eve were both naked and unashamed. From the point when Adam and Eve sin throughout the rest of the Bible, nakedness is almost always connected to shame. So rather than admitting they are broken and beaten by the work of the enemy, Adam and Eve covered up.

Do you remember when your kids were little? What was the first thing they did when you got them out of the bath? That's right- they ran naked all over the house. I have never met a child that did not do that, and if yours are like mine, they could not care less who is at the house. If the President of the United States is over for dinner and the kids are getting out of the bath, look out. Children are never concerned about being seen for what they really are; as time progresses, we teach them that nakedness is shameful. At some point, hopefully before they get into junior high, we teach them that it is not appropriate to run around the house naked. We teach them how to cover-up. Now I am not condoning streaking, but I want you to see how this exact principle has kept us from admitting our own spiritual brokenness over time.

We have taken the same approach with the Lord, with each other, with our families, especially inside the church. It is has become taboo to admit our brokenness or to be honest and forthright about the walls coming down in our lives. The enemy has convinced us to cover-up. He knows that until we are honest before a Holy God with the "naked truth" of our existence we will never be restored. How can we ever start the process of rebuilding until we first admit that things are broken? We can't. How will we ever be agents of healing for the broken generations following us? We won't. Listen to me, the God of the universe sent His only Son to die on a cross to rescue us, to restore us, to redeem us, and to rebuild us. We are not a people in Christ that have to cover up any longer. We do not have to stay in the dark and allow the enemy to have his way with our lives.

*But you are a chosen people, a royal priesthood, a holy nation, a people belonging to God, that you may declare the praises of Him who **called you out of darkness into His wonderful light.** Once you were not a people, but now you are the people of God; once you had not received mercy, but now you have received mercy. 1 Peter 2:9-10*

Do you see it? We do not have to hide. We do not have to fake it. We have been called out of the darkness into the wonderful light. We have been given mercy. We can come to our Father in the shame of our brokenness and find mercy and healing. We have been given Jesus- our Victor and Savior. Do you remember one of the last things the soldiers around Jesus did to Him after they brutally nailed Him to a nasty wooden cross? John 19:23-24 tells us that they stripped Him naked and rolled dice to see who would get His clothes. But why would they do that? It was a fulfillment of the prophecy in Psalms twenty-two, and it was for the purpose of shaming

Him. They shamed Him for you and me- He was shamed so that we would not have to be. We are clothed in Christ and never have to feel the sting of our shameful nakedness again. Just as Paul encourages the church at Galatia, we must realize that we too *"are all sons of God through faith in Christ Jesus, for all who were baptized into Christ have **clothed [ourselves] with Christ** (Galatians 3:26-27).*

We make the cross small and the sacrifice insignificant when we choose to stay in the dark and not be honest before a holy God. He stands ready to help us rebuild the spiritual walls. He desires to save that which is lost and restore that which is broken, but we have to be honest before Him and recognize our need for restoration. We are past the point in our nation, in our families, in our churches, where we can just put on the "face" and pretend like the condition of the spiritual walls is "fine." We must be willing to recognize that the "state of our union" is desperate and broken.

Right now, some of you reading this are truly struggling with an addiction that is tearing your family apart. Some of you are on the verge of calling it quits in your marriage. Some of you feel disconnected from the God who saved you. Some of you are in the midst of a financial disaster. Some of you are at your wits end when it comes to the relationship with your teenager. But on the outside looking in, the world would never know you are falling apart at the seams, especially those inside the church. Jesus knows, and He stands ready to help you rebuild. He is interceding for you, your family, your marriage, and your children right now. He stands ready to rescue the spiritual Orphas of America, but He will not move to rescue us until we first admit we are lost and in need of a Savior.

The children of America are spiritually dying and the best we can do is dress up real nice for Jesus, put on the face, and endure one more day? No, we cannot allow the enemy one more victory. We have a Savior- He is Jesus. He is waiting for us to recognize and admit our own brokenness. I want you to take this opportunity to look inside, to look around, and answer these questions before the Lord. What is the "naked truth" about your life, your marriage, your family, your church, your city, and your country? Is your walk with the Lord intimate? Is your marriage everything God said it should be? What is the truth about the spiritual state of your children, your neighbor's children? Is your church meeting the needs of the lost and destitute? Is your everyday "face" much different than your Sunday morning "face?"

This is an Emergency

By definition a **state of emergency** is *a governmental declaration that may suspend certain normal functions of government, alert citizens to alter their normal behaviors, or order government agencies to implement emergency preparedness plans. It can also be used as a rationale for suspending civil liberties. Such declarations usually come during a time of natural disaster, during periods of civil unrest, or following a declaration of war.*

If you are a parent, schoolteacher, youth or children's pastor, pastor, coach, social worker, or anyone who works with the children and young people of America let me ask you this question: "For our children, is this or is this not a *state of emergency?*" Time and again when speaking with adult groups, I ask this question and often times the general response is a quiet shoulder shrug, but when I ask this question specifically to those who spend every waking moment with the children of our country, the answer is emphatic and often tearful. THIS IS A STATE OF EMERGENCY!!! Week after week, I stand in front of a generation of young people who are broken and beaten by the world we have created for them. I could tell you story after story of the spiritual Orphas I meet everyday, and I feel certain those of you involved with our young people could do the same, but we need The

Church, the people of God, to acknowledge this truth. We must sound the alarm, *alert the citizens of the body to alter our normal behaviors, suspend our personal liberties,* and respond with urgency.

Listen to the words of the song forever playing in my mind. It was written by a Christian recording artist named Leeland who was only seventeen when he released it. "Tears of the Saints" was nominated for two Dove Awards in 2008, but what makes it noteworthy is the truth, honesty, and desperation of its words:

*There are many prodigal sons. On our city streets
they run. Searching for shelter.
There are homes broken down. People's hopes have
fallen to the ground from failures.*
This is an emergency!

*There are tears from the saints for the lost
and unsaved.
We're crying for them come back home.
We're crying for them come back home.
And all your children will stretch out their hands
and pick up the crippled man.
Father, we will lead them home. Father,
we will lead them home.*

*There are schools full of hatred. Even churches have
forsaken love and mercy.*
***May we see this generation in its state of
desperation for Your glory?***
This is an emergency!

I was so moved the first time I heard this song because I knew it was the desperate cry not of some cultural "expert," but of a young man who was living in the exact culture we have been called to change. He is sounding the alarm. This is an emergency- our children are in a state of spiritual desperation. Our homes are broken, our children have been abandoned, our families are falling apart, and our leaders have failed us. Can you see it? Just look around, read the newspaper, get on the internet, watch an hour of cable television, spend one lunch hour at your local junior high; do whatever it takes but please do not pretend that everything is "fine." It is too late and the situation too grave for our trained response. We must start dealing with the spiritual reality of our country.

This is not a call for us to react with panic or fear because we know, even in our most desperate state, the God we serve is on the throne. We must, however, respond with honesty and urgency. Until we recognize the severity of our depravity, we will never understand our need for a Savior who is capable of overcoming the greatest of tragedies- SIN. We need our Savior.

"Hello, my name is "The Children of America," and I am broken, beaten, tattered, and torn. Please help me."

You say, 'I am rich; I have acquired wealth and do not need a thing.' **But you do not realize that you are wretched, pitiful, poor, blind, and naked.** *I counsel you to buy from me gold refined in the fire, so you can become rich; white clothes to wear, so you can cover your shameful nakedness; salve to put on your eyes, so you can see. Revelation 3:17-18*

Section Three

Responsibility

Chapter Four

Connect the Dots

About two years ago I was reading the Bible through in chronological order, when God opened my eyes to something in the scripture that has burdened my heart since. He connected the dots for me in a way that humbled me and broke me in half. It was obvious that there was a principle in the Bible that pointed to how one generation has a spiritual responsibility to the next, but I was floored to see it so blatantly in black and white.

Let me set up the scripture for you. The book of Deuteronomy was written by Moses and was the last book of what is referred to as the Pentateuch- the first five books of the Bible, which include the laws and decrees that God gave His people before they entered the Promised Land. Deuteronomy locates the people of Israel in a place called Moab, which is where the Jordan River flows into the Dead Sea. After 400 years of enslavement to Pharaoh in Egypt, God calls Moses to lead them out. God previously made a covenant with Abraham promising that He was going to give his descendants, the Israelites, the land of Canaan- a land flowing with milk and honey. After a bunch of griping, whining, and wandering the desert for forty years, the people of Israel prepare to enter the Promised Land. Deuteronomy is written as the final instructions before the people of God enter the land. Listen carefully to the instructions God gives His people in Deuteronomy Chapter six:

*These are the commands, decrees, and laws the LORD your God directed me to teach you to observe in the land that you are crossing the Jordan to possess, **so that you, your children, and their children after them may fear the LORD your God as long as you live by keeping all His decrees and commands that I give you, and so that you may enjoy long life.** Hear, O Israel, and be careful to obey so that it may go well with you and that you may increase greatly in a land flowing with milk and honey, just as the LORD, the God of your fathers, promised you.*

*Hear, O Israel: The LORD our God, the LORD is one. Love the LORD your God with all your heart and with all your soul and with all your strength. These commandments that I give you today are to be upon your hearts. **Impress them on your children. Talk about them when you sit at home and when you walk along the road, when you lie down and when you get up.** Tie them as symbols on your hands and bind them on your foreheads. Write them on the doorframes of your houses and on your gates.*

In the future, when your son asks you, "What is the meaning of the stipulations, decrees and laws the LORD our God has commanded you?" tell him: "We were slaves of Pharaoh in Egypt, but the LORD brought us out of Egypt with a mighty hand. *Before our eyes the LORD sent miraculous signs and wonders—great and terrible—upon Egypt and Pharaoh and his whole household. But He brought* *us out from there to bring us in and give us the land that He promised on oath to our forefathers. The LORD commanded us to obey all these decrees and to fear the LORD our God, so that we might always prosper and be kept alive, as is the case today. And if we are careful to obey all this law before the LORD our God, as He has commanded us; that will be our righteousness." Deuteronomy 6:1-9, 20-25*

These are the very words of God to the people of Israel. He is placing on them the responsibility of ensuring that the generations who follow will know about the great things He has accomplished for them. He is calling the leaders, fathers, mothers, big brothers, and sisters to instruct the next generation in His ways. He is imploring them to teach their children the decrees and laws of the Lord- teach them His commandments, when they get up, when they sit down, when they are walking on the road. Deuteronomy six is not the only chapter filled with these instructions, in fact, the entire book of Deuteronomy is full of this mandate for the people of Israel. "Whatever you do, when you get into the land flowing with milk and honey and things are great there, do not forget to tell your children who I am and teach them to follow me." In the thirty-first chapter of Deuteronomy, as Moses is preparing to die, he makes one last effort to make sure that the people understand what is at stake. Listen to his declaration.

*Assemble the people—men, women, children, and the aliens living in your towns—so they can listen and learn to fear the LORD your God and follow carefully all the words of this law. **Their children, who do not know this law, must hear it and learn to fear the LORD your God** as long as you live in*

the land you are crossing the Jordan to possess."
Deuteronomy 31:12-13

Moses understands that the only way for the children of the next generation to know God is by learning about Him from the generation before them. This is called *generational discipleship* and is a principal found throughout the Bible. The book of Deuteronomy ends with the death of Moses and the changing of the guard for the leadership of Israel. Joshua, by Moses' side since the escape from Egypt, is now about to lead God's people into the land God promised them. Joshua has proven himself time and again as a faithful servant of the Lord and a valiant warrior. He leads the people through the Jordan River, around the walls of Jericho, and into numerous battles until the land belongs to the people of Israel. Just before his death, Joshua gathers the generation of elders and leaders to remind them again of the miracles and mandates of the Lord (Joshua 24). Unfortunately, somewhere along the way, the "elders who outlived Joshua" dropped the ball.

I want you to see exactly what happened after the people entered the land they were given by God:

After Joshua had dismissed the Israelites, they went to take possession of the land, each to his own inheritance. The people served the LORD throughout the lifetime of Joshua and of the elders who outlived him and who had seen all the great things the LORD had done for Israel. Joshua son of Nun, the servant of the LORD, died at the age of a hundred and ten. And they buried him in the land of his inheritance, at Timnath Heres in the hill country of Ephraim, north of Mount Gaash. **After that whole generation had been gathered to their fathers, another generation grew up, who knew neither the LORD nor what He had done for Israel. Then the Israelites did evil in** *the eyes of the LORD and served the Baals. They forsook the LORD, the God of their fathers, who had brought them out of Egypt. They followed and worshiped various gods of the peoples around them. They provoked the LORD to anger because they forsook Him and served Baal and the Ashtoreths.* In His anger against Israel, the LORD handed them over to raiders who plundered them. He sold them to their enemies all around, whom they were no longer able to resist. Whenever Israel went out to fight, the hand of the LORD was against them to defeat them, just as He had sworn to them. *They were in great distress.* Judges 2:6-19

Look at verse ten again. *After that whole generation had been gathered to their fathers, another generation grew up, who knew neither the LORD nor what He had done for Israel.*

Back in Deuteronomy, Joshua and the people of his generation were given a mandate from the Lord to teach and instruct the next generation in the ways of the Lord. Joshua did his part it seems, but it is clear the "elders that outlived him" did not. The text is clear that the generations following the "elders that outlived" Joshua had neither knowledge of the laws of the Lord nor what He had done for their forefathers. The results of the negligence of the elders are horrifying. The next generation quickly turns and worships the gods of the Canaanites. Apparently, the Canaanites are quick to teach them about their gods while the generation of Israelites who saw the one true God deliver them from the hand of Pharaoh, part the Jordan River, and crush Jericho remained silent.

I do not want you to hear want I am not saying. This adulterous generation that follows Joshua made a conscious choice to turn and serve the gods of those around them, but how could they follow a God they knew nothing about? How could they obey laws they did not understand or worship a God they had never heard of? How is it that they did not know about Pharaoh, the plagues, the death of the firstborn in Egypt, the parting of the Red Sea, the manna, or the water from the rock? God knew the comfort of the Promised Land would be detrimental to the spiritual health of His people. He took special care in warning them to teach their children and their children's children about the awesome things He had done for them and about His laws and decrees, but the elders did not heed His instructions. Somewhere along the way they stopped discipling the next generation, and the enemy quickly destroyed them.

This is a major turning point in the history of the nation of Israel, and eventually leads to the destruction of the city of God and captivity for the people of God. This is the pattern that leads to the walls being broken down in the days of Nehemiah. One generation refuses to disciple the next generation. This starts a trend in the nation of Israel that changes everything for the future generations of God's people. Let me connect the dots.

I have been traveling around the country for ten years spending almost every waking moment with the next generation of Americans. Here are a few things I have discovered:

Twelve year olds are not producing pornography for the internet.

Children are not making PG-13 movies full of foul language, violence, and sex.

They are not making and trafficking drugs into our country.

They are not voting on legislation allowing same sex marriage and abortion.

They are not producing MTV.

They are not divorcing one another at record numbers.

They are not working sixty hours a week and neglecting themselves.

They are not choosing to drag themselves to live with mom's new boyfriend.

They are not dropping themselves off at the mall for hours unattended.

They are not in charge of the schools they endure everyday.

They are definitely not filling our pulpits with a false gospel.

. . . All of those things are being done by adults.

Listen. Our children are not the ones breaking our homes in half- we are. They are not the ones filling the streets with the drugs they are hooked on- we are. They are not creating those violent video games that get the blame for every murder and suicide- we are. In a testimony before United States House of Representatives entitled "The Obesity Crisis in America" in 2003, Surgeon General Dr. Richard Carmona stated, "Our children did not create this problem. Adults did. Adults increased the portion size of children's meals, developed the games and television that children find spellbinding, and chose the sedentary lifestyles that our children emulate. **So adults must take the lead in solving this problem.**"

Our children are dying from diseases caused by obesity because we have failed them. The same is true for their spirituality. They are not tearing down the spiritual walls of our country- we are, and at some point we have to take some responsibility for the world we have built for them. We cannot continue to lead in these directions and then expect the results to be different than what we are experiencing right now. We are deciding for them, and a proper understanding of that should change everything about how we live our lives.

Today in our country, there are billions of dollars being spent trying to undo the damage we have done generation after generation to the planet on which we live. Our fear is that if we do not start making better decisions when it comes to the fuel we use or what we do with our soda cans, then our children and their children will be living on a melting planet consumed by trash. **The truth is, however, if we do not start making better *spiritual* decisions as a generation, then the corrosion of the Earth will be the least of our children's problems.** We are becoming more and more conscious of how our decisions effect the ozone layer and less and less conscious about how they effect the spiritually of our own children. Where is that campaign? Where are the television commercials? Where are the billboards?

I recently received a letter in the mail from Leonardo DiCaprio (the actor) about the plight of the polar bears in Alaska. Here is a quote from the letter, "The polar bear is sending us a desperate S.O.S. You and I can no longer turn our backs on these warning sings—even if our political and corporate leaders keep denying the truth.[10]" The letter went on to say that over one million Americans already supported the movement to save the polar bears. Listen, I have nothing against the polar bears or those who are trying to help them, but our priorities are so incredibly backwards. Our children are "sending us a desperate S.O. S. and we can no longer turn our backs on these warning signs."

We place more value on the extinction of animals and less and less on the extinction of the morality of our people. God bless the polar bears, but right now in this country we are in need of God's blessing for the children of America. I hate that the decisions we have made from generation to generation have put our Earth and its animals at risk, but more than anything, I hate that our spiritual decisions have put the children of America in incredible danger. The truth is that even the disintegration of our planet and our animals is a direct result of sin, and I do not mean failing to recycle. Sin broke our world not just in a spiritual sense, but in a literal sense as well, and the creation of God cries out for His return that it too might be redeemed (Roman 8:19-22). I am all for being "green" but if we truly want to change the environment, we must begin by assuming responsibility for the spiritual mess we have made for the coming generations of American children.

Week after week, I hear the stories of our children, and I remember as a youth pastor how upset I would get knowing that no matter how much I poured into certain students, they would continually come back to me empty because their home life would suck the life of God right out of them. If you are one who deals with the young people of America daily, you know exactly what I am talking about. All that you can do for them in a day or even a week can be undone in twenty minutes in their own homes. I am not letting the young people of America off the hook for their actions because one day they themselves will answer for the way they lived this life and they will not be able to blame us, but I cannot let us off the hook either.

We are supposed to be teaching our children and their children about the awesome salvation God brought us through Jesus. We are supposed to be teaching them about the laws and decrees of the Lord- the very Word of God. We are supposed to be living out lives in front of them that mirrors who God is in this world. We are supposed to be protecting them from the flaming darts of the enemy not opening the door for him to come in to rape and murder them. We are supposed to be training them in righteousness and covering them in prayer. We are responsible for the decisions we make, and we must recognize the spiritual part we play today in what our world will look like tomorrow.

Like the generation of "elders that outlived Joshua," we have failed to teach the next generation about the laws and decrees of the God of Abraham. We have failed to teach them about how God rescued us from the tyranny of the enemy. How can we expect them to trust a God they know nothing about? How can we expect them to honor the commandments of God if we have not lived out those things for them to see? Can you see it? We are the spiritual walls around the next generation designed by God to protect them from the enemy and equip them to live out the kingdom of God. We are the gates by which the world has access to our children. We are the walls; we are the gates, and we are broken. The results of our negligence are clear for all to see- the children of the next generation know nothing of the things of God or what He has done for them. This is our responsibility. It is yours and it is mine.

I have a friend who is a principal at one of our local junior high schools. He cares genuinely for the students that attend his school, and he desires for them to grow up with a solid education and become good productive citizens. About nine years ago, I showed up at his school one day and asked if I could come and eat lunch with students once day. He was obviously skeptical and asked many questions about my intentions, making sure to explain that I could not go in there and preach about God. I assured him that I would behave, and he graciously gave me permission. We built a friendship during my time as a youth pastor, and he invited me to serve on what is called a site-based committee for his school. We meet every month or so and talk about where the students are in school, life, and then we sit around a table and try to figure out a way to make a difference in their lives.

As I was doing research for this book, I stopped by one day to visit with him. We started talking about the book, and when I got to this point, his eyes lit up. I said, "What? What just happened?" He stopped me and with tears in his eyes, he said, "Kevin, the greatest challenge we face with this generation of young people is finding adults in their lives who will love and support them. This year alone, my staff and I have done 200 home visits to homes where we know students do not have a solid example. We went there hoping that if we could make a relationship with someone in their lives, then maybe we could influence them to take up the responsibility of seeing that student do well in school, in life. I know that you feel inadequate to write this book, but I implore you to please keep saying this one thing. We need the generation that is rearing our children to recognize that they are the single biggest influence in the way their children live life." My friend might not be able to see the correlation between Deuteronomy six and Judges two, but he can certainly recognize the responsibility we have to the coming generations. I want take it a step further so you can see exactly how God designed this process to work.

Chapter Five

God is a Gardener, So Are We

*Then God said, "Let the land produce vegetation: seed-bearing plants and trees on the land that bear fruit with seed in it, according to their various kinds." And it was so. The land produced vegetation: **plants bearing seed according to their kinds and trees bearing fruit with seed in it according to their kinds.** And God saw that it was good. Genesis 1:11-12*

When God built the planet, He started with a garden for a reason. He created the plants to be seed-bearing plants each according to its kind, and He said it was good. Peach trees would produce peach trees and bananas trees would give way to more banana trees. This was His way of filling the Earth with the plants of each kind: tree, fruit, seed-new tree of the same kind. God liked this system, so when He created Adam and Eve, He took the exact same approach. He created them in His own image, and He told them to be *fruitful* and increase in number and to fill the Earth (Genesis 1:27-28). He created Adam to carry a seed that would produce another man (fruit) in the image of Adam, in the image of God. Procreation was about filling the Earth with the image of God.

Our offspring are to look like us, and we are to look like Jesus. This continues until they look like Jesus and produce another crop, another generation who looks like them. This planting and reaping language is found throughout the Bible to the extent that God declares that He identifies His children by the fruits they produce (Matthew 7:15-23). God is a gardener, and so are you. We have a major role to play in the next crop- the upcoming generation. Whether we like it or not, what we plant will grow.

> *Do not be deceived: God cannot be mocked. A man reaps what he sows. The one who sows to please his sinful nature, from that nature will reap destruction; the one who sows to please the Spirit, from the Spirit will reap eternal life. Galatians 6:7-9*

One day when I was a youth pastor, I got a phone call from the mother of one of our students in the youth group. She was livid and wanted to come by and talk with me about her son. When she arrived, she instantly started going on and on about how bad her son was and how he was aloof, distant, and disrespectful. Finally, she came to a solid conclusion. She said, "And the thing that frustrates me the most is how non-committal he is." I am not known for pulling punches, but as soon as the sound hit my vocal cords, I knew I was about to say something I would probably want to take back at some point. I looked over the desk at her, and as gently as I could, I said, "Well Mrs. Smith, all of those things are valid issues that your son needs to work on, but with all due respect, since you had him, you have been married and divorced two times. Commitment is not something that your son knows a lot about." As much as it hurt me to say, and probably for this mother to hear, the example this boy was watching everyday taught him that commitment was not important. He was just following his example. God will not be mocked, what we plant will grow.

It blows my mind how many times in the Bible we see this exact same scenario play out in the lives of the characters there. From generation to generation, children often repeat the exact same sins as their parents. I am not talking about "generational sin," as some would call it, because each generation has a choice in what they become, but do not be fooled, our decisions effect their decisions. Let me give you an example.

I hate divorce. There are too many reasons to list, and we will discuss this in depth later, but I will say this now: The destruction of the family in America, especially the Christian family, is the single leading cause of the spiritual epidemics we are experiencing generation after generation. The enemy is destroying the mechanism that God created for discipleship- he is killing us from the inside out. A fellow named Nicholas H. Wolfinger, an associate professor of sociology at the University of Utah, has written a book called, <u>Understanding the Divorce Cycle</u>. In the book Wolfinger asserts that, "Growing up in a divorced family greatly increases the chances of ending one's own marriage, a phenomenon called the divorce cycle or the **intergenerational transmission** of divorce. The divorce cycle, in short, can be thought of as a cascade. Ending a marriage starts a cycle that threatens to affect increasing numbers of people over time, a sobering thought in an era when half of all new marriages fail.[11]"

Intergenerational transmission of divorce- Did you notice that term? The secular experts have even come up with a word for exactly what the Bible has been pointing to for centuries: What you plant will grow. The studies to support Wolfinger's claims are numerous; some go so far as to say that spouses who are both children of divorced parents are **three times** more likely to divorce than couples who both hail from intact families. There are similar statistics and studies out there that point to the same intergenerational transmission of physical abuse, substance abuse, and other related issues. The point is this: if we plant apple trees, apple trees will grow. If we plant divorce, divorce will grow; if we plant profanity, profanity will grow; if we plant godlessness, godlessness is most certainly going to grow.

> *Sow for yourselves righteousness, reap the fruit of unfailing love, and break up your unplowed ground; for it is time to seek the LORD, until He comes and showers righteousness on you. **But you have planted wickedness, you have reaped evil**, you have eaten the fruit of deception. Hosea 10:12-13*

One of the best ways for us to know what we have planted as a generation is to look around at what is growing in the next one. If you want to know what a farmer planted, just check out his crop. It seems simple enough, but think about that for a moment- What is growing in the generations following us? It is pretty frightening. You may be saying to yourself, "Well, I certainly did not plant those things in the next generation." That may be true, and I hope I have not planted some of the things I see, but not only are we responsible to plant, we are also accountable for what gets planted. Beyond planting, we are called to be the spiritual wall against what the enemy is planting. Just as a responsible gardener must do, we are called to cultivate, fertilize, water, and protect the soil that is the life of the next generation. We may not be able to shut down the pornography industry or end the madness on television, but we can certainly make an effort to protect our children from these seeds of evil.

I am not saying tie them up in their room and never let them be light in a dark world, but I am saying we must quit leaving them alone in the darkness of the world to fend for themselves. Here is a perfect example. We are all aware that the Internet is a porthole to some of the vilest things on our planet. So why in the world would we leave our children alone in their rooms with it? Think about it. If you knew your neighbor was a demented child molester would you allow your children to hang out at his house? Of course not, so why would we allow our children to surf around in a world full of demented child molesters?

If you knew me, you would not label me "legalistic," but if someone were to think about planting something evil in my children, they would be hearing from me, and I do not mean by email. I cannot apologize for that- we should not have to- God has given us a responsibility to our children, to the next generation. You and I are called to protect our children, the next generation, from the flaming darts of the enemy. We are the spiritual walls around them and the gates by which everything must pass in order to get into their lives. If the walls are broken and gates are left wide open, and our children are without the ability to defend themselves, the results are horrifying. If you do not believe me, just pick up a copy of the newspaper.

We have to learn to say, "No, you cannot eat that, you cannot watch that, you cannot listen to that, you cannot date him, you cannot go there and here is why: Because we love you and we have a spiritual responsibility in your life." We have to do the hard things even when it hurts. We must not allow the enemy to plant the evil of our world in them at will. We must reach our generation with this message. The spiritual decisions that we make as adult leaders have a huge effect on the generations that are following us. We are leaving a spiritual legacy with them, and right now that legacy is not what God would have it be.

Defend the Vulnerable

There is something we must understand about the character and heart of God. One thing we know for certain is that God takes very seriously the way in which His people treat the weak and the vulnerable. He often judges His people, not for bringing the wrong sacrifice or worshipping on the wrong day, but on their commitment to protect and defend the widow, the children, and the orphaned. Listen to this rebuke God gives the people of Israel through the prophet Isaiah:

> *Hear the word of the LORD, you rulers of Sodom; listen to the law of our God, you people of Gomorrah! "The multitude of your sacrifices—what are they to me?" says the LORD."I have more than enough of burnt offerings, of rams and the fat of fattened animals; I have no pleasure in the blood of bulls and lambs and goats. When you come to appear before me, who has asked this of you, this trampling of my courts? Stop bringing meaningless offerings! Your incense is detestable to me. New Moons, Sabbaths, and convocations—I cannot bare your evil assemblies. Your New Moon festivals and your appointed feasts my soul hates. They have become a burden to me; I am weary of bearing them. When you spread out your hands in prayer, I will hide my eyes from you; even if you offer many prayers, I will not listen. Your hands are full of blood; wash and make yourselves clean. Take your evil deeds out of my sight!* ***Stop doing wrong, learn to do right! Seek justice, encourage the oppressed. Defend the cause of the fatherless, plead the case of the widow.*** *Isaiah 1:10-17*

God is angry with His people and compares them by name to the world-renowned sinners in Sodom and Gomorrah- two cities that He himself destroyed by fire in the days of Abraham. But why is God so angry with His people? Because they put on a good show making sacrifices and they do "the church thing" really well, but they do not protect the weak and vulnerable. Children are the weakest and most vulnerable of all people. They are defenseless against the spiritual attacks of the enemy and do not have the ability to defend themselves against the lies of the world. They are reliant upon those called to protect them; they are reliant upon us. This is the heart of God- defend the cause of the weak. God tells His people to quit gathering before Him with a suit and song, and learn to do what is right. We must defend those who cannot defend themselves.

I have to be careful here because more and more I find myself angry at certain adults that have no regard for the junk they are planting in the lives of their children or what they are allowing the world to plant. For the longest time, I felt like my passion for this subject was some sort of the judgmental self-righteous sin, but over the past few years, God has convinced me that this anger is simply His Spirit inside me. He is angry. Obviously, not all anger is godly, but when we study the Word and see what angers God we have the freedom, even the responsibility, to be angry over the things that anger the heart of our Father in Heaven.

I recently coached my seven-year-old son's flag football team. Week after week, we had an issue with the coaches of other teams cursing out loud during the games. Several times I had to ask grown men to watch their language around my team. Not all of them took it with a smile, but I cannot apologize for trying to defend the lives of the children God put in my care. Without someone interceding for them, my boys, and the boys of the other teams, are without the ability to defend themselves. We must realize the words we say, our attitudes, prejudices, and personal convictions are all seeds we are planting in the lives of the next generation. We must also realize those around us are planting those things in the lives of our children as well.

The worst thing I can imagine happening on this planet is an adult harming a child. Think about it: When you hear of an adult physically abusing or molesting a child, does it make you angry? Of course it does because you recognize that children are defenseless and vulnerable. Should we not consider it an even greater travesty that our children are being left to fend for themselves spiritually? In no way am I diminishing the devastation of physical abuse to a child, but it is their spiritual understanding that determines their place in eternity. We must fight with the same fervor we would to protect children from physical abuse in defending them spiritually. We must do what is right.

I find myself in front of students on a weekly basis who are living through the most horrific things. Time after time they tell me about how their home life is completely broken. "I live with my dad mostly, but he has a new girlfriend, so I have been staying with my mom this semester." "My folks are constantly at each other, so I spend most of my time in my room listening to music or on the Internet." The stories go on and on and with each one, I say the same thing. I tell them how they have a chance to change the spiritual legacy of their family forever. They can choose not to live out the life they have seen modeled. Every once in a while, one of them does, and by the grace of God, they will change the spiritual legacy for their children and their children's children, but it breaks my heart that most of them will not. Without the intercession of the Lord in their lives, they will become products of the things planted in them and planters of those very same things. For the most part, young people respond to what has been planted in them in two ways: they become what they have seen modeled or they despise everything about what is modeled. If they have an alcoholic dad, then they either become an alcoholic or they despise everything about alcohol. The problem is, however, the second group is the exception and not the rule.

I have cried myself to sleep many times wrestling with the Lord trying to figure out how I can be an instrument of change. The product of this struggle is the realization that if I want to be a catalyst for spiritual revival in the coming generations, I have to help the current generations recognize their spiritual responsibility. I have to be willing to encourage and strengthen those who are in a position to lead. It is not enough to simply continue to treat the symptoms of the disease of sin in our children; we must get to the root of the epidemic. If you have children of any age, you must recognize your spiritual responsibility to them. You are the keeper of the garden that is their life; you are there to plant the things of God into them and pull out the weeds of the world.

My failures are way too many to recount, and I seem to be inventing new ones with each child God instructs me to lead. None of us are any man's judge and all of us are light years from perfect, so please do not misunderstand this fervor. My goal is to encourage those who are fighting everyday for the souls of the next generation and to awaken those that are tearing down the spiritual walls by ignoring their responsibility in the process. For too long we have been apologizing ourselves into saying nothing at all. I cannot do that this time around. The stakes are too high and the children of the next generation have names and faces that I cannot forget.

You and I are to be keepers of the garden that is the next generation. The results of our efforts are not dependent on us, but we are responsible to give them everything they need to live out the call of God. What are you planting in the lives of the next generation? What are you allowing to be planted in the lives of our children?

From Responsible to Accountable

Do you remember the priest in the Old Testament named Eli in the book of I Samuel? Eli had two sons whom the Bible tells us were "wicked men, who had no regard for the Lord." Listen to this scripture about Eli and his sons.

> *And the LORD said to Samuel: "See, I am about to do something in Israel that will make the ears of everyone who hears of it tingle. At that time I will carry out against Eli everything I spoke against his family-from beginning to end. **For I told him that I would judge his family forever because of the sin he knew about; his sons made themselves contempt-ible, and he failed to restrain them.** Therefore, I swore to the house of Eli, the guilt of Eli's house will never be atoned for by sacrifice or offering."*
> *I Samuel 3:11-14*

Eli is not punished because his sons are wicked, but he is held accountable for not spiritually parenting them. He knew about the sin they were involved with, but he did not restrain them. Listen, I need you to understand this. Every person will answer to the God of Heaven and Earth for the life they have lived and will not be able to say on that day, "Well, my mom and dad were divorced, so I acted wickedly." The point is our generation like many before us is failing to give the next generation everything they need to walk in the ways of the Lord. We are not only responsible to lead the next generation, we are held accountable for how we lead them. Both Eli and his sons endured the wrath of God. His sons are punished for being wicked, but Eli is punished for knowing they were wicked and doing nothing to lead them in righteousness. We must recognize the areas where we have failed the next generation so we can change the way we lead them. If God has blessed you with children, you are accountable to parent them in the ways of the Lord. It is the most important job you have on the planet.

Contract Labor

I need to make one last thing clear for all of us who are parents before I involve the rest of the family of God in this process. As parents, we are both responsible and accountable for the lives of our children. Over the past few decades we have bought into this "contract labor" type of parenting. Just like many of today's homebuilders, we contract out our responsibilities for every area of our children's lives. We expect the government to feed them, the schools to educate them, the coaches to teach them the game, the police to protect them, and the youth pastor or children's pastor to train them to walk with Jesus. If your son does not know how to read, that is your responsibility. If your daughter is spending time with a young man who is a threat to physically or spiritually dishonor her, you should be the one to recognize it and step in to put a stop to it. If your son cannot throw or kick a ball, it is your job to spend some time with him in the backyard. If your daughter is confused about what salvation in Christ truly is, you should be available and able to answer those questions.

Our children are not killing each other because of lax gun laws; they are killing each other because we have failed to lead them in the Lord. Our teenagers are not having premarital sex because the school system has failed to educate them about sex; they are sexually active because we have not taken the time to truly teach them the value of true purity and to protect them from the sin that so easily entangles. Our children do not despise going to church just because the youth pastor does not talk to them or the preaching is boring; it could be they despise going to church because every Sunday morning our attitude says that we do too. I am not so naïve to think we can keep our children from every danger or all the tares of sin, but we can honor God by being involved in every step of their spiritual upbringing. I recognize that God does not need our help when it comes to rearing our children; in fact, He does not need our help with anything, but like the "elders that outlived Joshua," He has placed on us the responsibility of teaching them how to walk with Him in every area of their lives.

Chapter Six

Who is Following Me?

I see some guys sitting in the back row who have no children left at home wondering how this applies to them, so let me broadened the scope of the challenge. We have seen the mandate given by Moses to the generation of Israelites about the next generation, so we understand that the principal is in tact for us. The gardening principal is a great revelation so let me set the bar a little higher so all of us can get a picture of our own responsibility to the next generation.

> *Then Jesus came to them and said, "All authority in Heaven and on Earth has been given to me. **Therefore go and make disciples** of all nations, baptizing them in the name of the Father and of the Son and of the Holy Spirit, and teaching them to obey everything I have commanded you. And surely I am with you always, to the very end of the age." Matthew 28:18-20*

We all know this one. This is what is called "The Great Commission." It is the mandate Jesus gives just before He ascends into Heaven to sit at the right hand of The Father. But what does it mean? Some of you have been asking yourself this question, "Why am I on this planet?" If you are a follower of King Jesus, then you exist on the planet to bring God glory by making disciples. This is the commission, the authoritative command of God for all those who consider themselves His followers. We are to make replicas of Jesus – Christians, but for a number of reasons we do not have time to discuss, (selfish ambition, laziness, pride, misunderstanding of scripture, corporate church model, idolatry, etc.) we have traded the making of disciples for the creation of converts. Rather than actually teaching the next generation how to follow God, we just ask them to raise their hand if they like Jesus and then we add them to the membership role.

Let me be gentle in this rebuke. God is not interested in how many members you have on the role at your "church." He is interested in your commitment to the discipleship of the next generation. This misunderstanding may be one of the greatest missteps of the American church. For far too long we have been connecting our ability to garnish "conversions" into a status marker for success, all the while, downplaying the actual call of God to make disciples.

We have to stop judging churches and ministries based on the number of people who show up to the Sunday morning Jesus production, and start judging them based on how effective they are at making life-giving, passionate, committed, followers of King Jesus. I am not saying we should not gather and proclaim the gospel of Jesus; we should preach the gospel to all nations, we should sing about Jesus, share communion in Jesus, love Jesus, tithe, and have the biggest crowd possible, but we must be willing to actually obey the commission of Jesus if we desire to advance His kingdom.

I was recently discussing this problem in the American church with a pastor friend of mine. When I asked him how big his church was, he said, "I have 199." I was a little confused because I know that is not the number of members in his church- it is a large, affluent church with a membership at least ten times that. I pressed him, and he explained that 199 is the number of people in his church who are true disciple-makers. You see, you cannot be considered a disciple until you are a disciple-maker. Here is why this discussion is so important to the conversation we are having about repairing the broken walls.

Not too long ago, I was watching a movie with my wife. The movie is about a radical Islamic group blowing up an American military base in the Middle East and the ensuing investigation into the crime by some military CSI types. There is a particular scene in the movie that overwhelmed me to the point of tears, but it is not the scene that seemed to grip those around us. As the Islamic radicals put the plan into motion, five or six men gather on a rooftop watching it all come together. It was obvious that there are three generations of one family of men gathered there. As the plan, eventually leading to the killing of hundreds of people begins to unfold on the streets below, the eldest of the men calls to what appears to be his grandson, and hands him the binoculars. With great joy and passion, he begins to explain to the young boy exactly what is unfolding. As if he is preparing the young boy to repeat the exact exercise the next day, he carefully tutors him through the details of the scheme.

I began to cry. God was speaking to me about what I was watching unfold. It was not just the realization of the oncoming evil that struck me; it was the incredible way in which evil was being carried from grandfather to father to grandson. One generation training the next generation to carry out the mission of their cause. The cause was no doubt evil, but the process of discipleship was powerful. It was not taking place in a classroom, or through a podcast, or even via a fill in the blank book study; it was taking place in life; in a moment on the roof.

As of today, our country is at war with a group of people who seem to be an unstoppable force. Their commitment, fervor, passion, and process of discipleship make them almost impossible to defeat, even with the greatest military in the world. They are serious about what they believe, serious about their walls, serious about their god, and serious about the discipleship of the next generation of terrorists- and they do it all for a god that does not exist. As I was watching this scene play out in the movie, my Spirit began to scream inside of me. "Kevin, you serve the one, true, living God, and your fervor to train the next generation of life-givers has in no way been equal to those making disciples of evil."

Then I realized the truth. Islamic radicals, Muslims, Buddhist, Mormons, and almost every other world religion that teaches outside of the truth of the Bible takes discipleship very seriously- American Christians do not. Something has to change. From the time their children are young, other faith groups teach, mold, train, and disciple with intention and conviction. They understand the future of their cause is only as strong as the next generation. We must open our eyes to this truth. There should not be a people on the planet who rival the passion and fervor with which we disciple our children because we serve the only God of Heaven and Earth. If we desire to see the spiritual walls of our country strong for future generations of Americans, we must begin to take the process of discipleship more seriously.

Discipleship done rightly is the most important tool we have for rebuilding the spiritual walls for the future generations in America.

We must get this right- all of us, not just parents, but all Christians. **If you call yourself a follower of God (a Christian), but you are not in the process of making disciples of King Jesus, you have not lived out the call of God on your life.** There are no exceptions. For those of you without children of your own or who have children that have already moved into adulthood, this statement still applies to you.

Follow this thought process with me. Discipleship is the arduous process by which we cultivate, plant, and grow the next generation of Christians in America. It is a selfless process that is often incredibly uncomfortable and difficult. You cannot fake your way through it, or just pop in a DVD and call it good. There are no shortcuts. Discipleship is not one hour a week spent eating donuts, drinking Starbucks and chatting about "how to manage your money with Jesus." These things are important, but we have to move the process of discipleship out of the partitioned off rooms of Sunday morning back into the homes and lives of Christian leaders. **We have to once again make discipleship more about** *followship* **than fellowship.** The call of Jesus to His disciples was, "Come and follow me," not "Come and visit me once a week."

Discipleship is more akin to apprenticeship than it is to the lecturer/student model. Jesus spent everyday with twelve guys for three years; they followed Him everywhere. The Hebrew word for disciple is talmidid, and the overall understanding of the process was not just to learn from your rabbi; the goal was to follow your rabbi until you become like him in every way. **Discipleship is not about the transferring of information; it is about the transformation of character.** Each of us has a spiritual responsibility to those following us. My son has a spiritual obligation to his younger sister. Why? She is following him. I do not care how old or young you are; if you are a follower of Jesus, you must begin to think in these terms- the next generation is counting on it. Here are two questions that we should be asking ourselves everyday:

Who is following me?
Where am I taking them?

Train Them in the Way They Should Go

As I was watching the scene in this movie unfold, I was struck with the precision and intention with which the grandfather instructs his grandson. He literally puts him through a training exercise on terrorism. He does not simply give him instructions on how to murder innocent people; he teaches him why, according to their beliefs, he should do so. He trains the young boy with passion, conviction, intention, and what he thinks is love. He instructs him to not just do as he does but to be like he is. **Discipleship is about training.** God's call on our lives is to train those who follow us to be like us, to be like Jesus. Here is a familiar scripture that offers us a true understanding of the heart of discipleship.

> *Train a child in the way he should go, and when he is old he will not turn from it.*
> *Proverbs 22:6*

I hear this scripture quoted when young people raised in the church find themselves living with the pigs, and I am grateful it is true; however, we often forget this scripture is an if/then conditional statement. *If* you train a child in the way he should go, *then* when he is old he will not turn from it. The problem is we are not training those following us in the way they should go. Think about the things we spend time and money on. We spend millions of dollars and countless hours a year to train our young boys to throw a baseball, kick a soccer ball, or catch a football, but when it comes to training them to walk with Jesus, the same cannot be said.

Can you imagine if we spent the same amount of time, energy, and resources on the spiritual training of those following us as we do on sports alone in this country? Sunday morning might become the rage that Monday night football is. Training takes an incredible amount of time, energy, effort, resources, knowledge, and intention. We must recognize that each of us has been called to train those who are following us to follow Jesus. We must also recognize that this call for trainers goes way beyond just parents; this call to discipleship is for anyone who calls themselves a follower of Jesus.

The Hammer

Let me give you a "life application" example for the training process we call discipleship. If your father is a roofer by trade, then as a boy, you may spend countless hours sitting on a roof next to your dad handing him nails and watching him hammer. Day after day you hand him nails until one day he hands you the hammer. The process of discipleship is just like that. The problem is that many of our children are sitting at home without anyone to train them, so when they finally get a shot at the hammer, they have no clue what to do with it. Think about it like this- If you get a new puppy, you can almost guarantee that at some point the puppy is going to soil your carpet or eat your couch. If he is not trained to do something different, he will continue to destroy your house not knowing that a different behavior is expected. He is not going to wake up one day a year down the road and decide, "Hey, you know what, I should probably do this outside." Sounds silly, but it makes perfect sense: you have to train him to go outside. In a similar manner, the young people of the next generation need to be trained to walk with Jesus.

Jesus personally taught the disciples how to be men of God, how to cast out demons, how to treat the sick, how to preach the word, how to love, how to be servants, how to tie their sandals, how to interpret prophecy, and how to die. When they got the hammer, they knew exactly what to do with it, and you and I should be glad because through these men, the gospel reached us thousands of years later on the other side of the planet. One disciple at a time, the gospel has traveled through space and time to reach us that we might use it to rescue the next generation via the exact same process.

In I Kings nineteen, God instructs the prophet Elijah to go find a young man named Elisha and anoint him as the next prophet of God. Elisha leaves everything and follows Elijah as his "prophet in training" until the time comes for God to take Elijah into glory. When God takes Elijah, He leaves for Elisha the cloak of his master, and Elisha knows exactly what to do with it. He walks up to the Jordan River, just as he saw Elijah do, and strikes the water with it. Just as it had for Elijah, the waters divide to the right and to the left for him to cross over (2 Kings 2:13-14). Elijah trains Elisha so when he receives the cloak he will know exactly what to do. In the end, Elisha does twice as many miraculous things as his teacher Elijah.

Can we say that about the generation we have been called to lead? Are they prepared to accomplish twice as much as we have in the Lord? Generations pass, but without discipleship the next one has no clue what to do with the hammer. With each break in the spiritual discipleship process, we move further away from the lives God has called us to lead. Our children do not need another big tent revival or strategically-packaged sermon series; they need to spend some time on the roof with men and women who know how to follow God with passion and conviction.

I hear young ladies all the time talking about how the "boys" of this generation have no idea how to treat a "lady." For the most part, I would have to agree, but why? It is simple really- they have had no training in how to treat a "lady." When I was a young boy, I remember specifically going to the mall with my mom and my three younger sisters. They would walk up to the door to the mall entrance and just stand there. At first I was like, "What are you doing women? Are we going in or not?" Then I realized they were waiting for me to open the door. We would have stood there all day had

I not opened the door. My mother was giving me a lesson in how to properly treat a woman that I would not have known otherwise. In the same manner, the young boys of America will not know either unless we train them. Let me be fair. I also get sick to my stomach at the way young women allow men to treat them. If you came to pick up one of my baby sisters for a date and you just drove up to the curb and honked; good luck, because the only people coming through that door would be my father or me telling you to get lost.

When I turned sixteen, my mom and dad bought me a car. It was a charcoal grey Mercury Topaz with the most hideous maroon interior, but that was not the worst part; it had four doors. When I asked my father why he bought me a car with four doors, his response was simple. He said, "I did not buy that car for you. I bought it for your sisters; you are just their driver." He was teaching me about discipleship. I was to be a part of the training process for my sisters. He expected me to be an example for them, and he made it clear what kind of example I was to be. I was to respect them, protect them, care for them, fight for them, and serve them. My father was training me how to treat a woman and training my sisters how they should expect to be treated. Why? So when we got the hammer we would know exactly what to do with it.

Worthy of Respect?

I want you to read this text with me out of Titus 2:1-8 so we can get an understanding of the requirements of God for those of us called to train the next generation.

*You must teach what is in accord with sound doctrine. Teach the older men to be temperate, **worthy of respect**, self-controlled, and sound in faith, in love and in endurance. Likewise, teach the older women to be reverent in the way they live, not to be slanderers or addicted to much wine, but to teach what* *is good. **Then they can train the younger women to love their husbands and children, to be self-controlled and pure, to be busy at home, to be kind, and to be subject to their husbands,** so that no one will malign the word of God. Similarly, encourage the young men to be self-controlled. **In everything set them an example by doing what is good.** In your teaching show integrity, seriousness and soundness of speech that cannot be condemned, so that those who oppose you may be ashamed because they have nothing bad to say about us.*

Paul is giving to his spiritual son Titus the mechanism by which disciples are to be made inside and outside of the church. There is much more here than just teaching Sunday school. He is imploring the older men to *train* the younger men and the older women to *train* the younger women. He also gives both the men and the women a set of standards for living and implores them to set an example for the next generation by doing what is good. Set an example. . . why? Because they will do as they have seen us do. They are looking for someone to follow, and if they are following us, then we should be following God.

Paul tells us that the older men are to be temperate, worthy of respect, self-controlled and sound in faith in love and endurance, and their teaching should show integrity, seriousness, and soundness of speech. Notice Paul does not tell the older men that they should *be respected;* he tells them to be *worthy of respect.* Let me see if I can use a fallacy of the current generation of young people to drive home the seriousness of our responsibilities inside this text. American teenagers seem to be very disrespectful. I spend thirty-two hours a day with students and can attest to their "lack of respect," but let's put it in context with this teaching. Have the men and women of our country shown themselves overall to be *worthy of respect?*

Think about it from the standpoint of the next generation. They have seen politicians, pastors, fathers, mothers, professional athletes, teachers, and coaches time after time say one thing and do another. They have endured lies and scandals from every position of authority. They have seen half the marriage promises in our country broken, and when the phone rings, they know it is another adult trying to sell them something they know is a scam. Every time they check their email, their inbox is full of promises they know others will not keep. Then there is the television evangelist with the Rolex and the big hair who is trying to convince the world to send him five bucks for a prayer cloth he says will cure their mom of cancer. Does that sound "worthy of respect" to you? Is it any wonder that the most popular word of the today's young people is, "Whatever!"?

There is a song that was made popular by the band, The Beastie Boys, when I was growing up called, "You Gotta Fight For Your Right to Party." There is a single line in the song that always struck me as a travesty. It says, "Your pops caught you smoking and said, 'NO WAY,' but that hypocrite smokes two packs a day." Worthy of respect?

I recognize we are fallible and prone to failure, but are we a generation worthy of respect? I could give you a list a mile long about the ideals and issues the next generation needs to fix- issues for which they will be held responsible, but I could also point to the birth of each issue in those called to be their examples -issues we will be held responsible for. Did you notice in all the instruction to the people of Titus' church, Paul only includes one line actually directed at the younger generation? Why? Because Paul understands the overwhelming importance of the example set by adults. "Generation Next" needs trainers who are respectful men and women of integrity committed to the process of discipleship. We need to stop complaining about the way the next generation acts and start living out the call of God on our lives so they will have an alternative example to the ones modeled by the world everyday. We must stop saying one thing and doing another, and begin the process of personal revival in our own hearts knowing that our revival is the key to their hope for one.

Chapter Seven

Understated Devastation

Here is the problem at the root of the true brokenness of the spiritual walls: The family in America is broken. There is a reason the enemy has worked so hard to destroy the structure of the Christian family. He hates disciples of King Jesus, and the family is the machine God invented to produce His disciples. When the machine is broken, it does not produce as it should. Listen to the revelations in this scripture about the heart of God concerning this very thing.

> *Another thing you do: You flood the LORD'S altar with tears. You weep and wail because He no longer pays attention to your offerings or accepts them with pleasure from your hands. You ask, "Why?" It is because the LORD is acting as the witness between you and the wife of your youth, because you have broken faith with her, though she is your partner, the wife of your marriage covenant. Has not [the LORD] made them one? In flesh and spirit they are His. And why one? **Because He was seeking godly offspring. So guard yourself in your spirit, and do not break faith with the wife of your youth. "I hate divorce,"** says the LORD God of Israel. . . Malachi 2:13-16*

God hates divorce, but why? The answer is found right here. He hates it because He made the man and woman physically and spiritually "one" for the purpose of producing godly offspring. The family was designed by God for the purpose of filling the whole Earth with His glory- to make disciples of King Jesus. Listen, if you are someone who has been through a divorce, the Lord does not hate you nor do I, but for too long we have been drawing fuzzy lines about this subject. This is truth. Divorce, when committed as sin, is like any other sin; it is forgiven by the blood of Jesus whose grace is sufficient for all sin; however, we must understand that it still has devastating spiritual consequences.

If you jump off a building with the intent to kill yourself, is that a sin? Of course it is. Is the penalty for that sin paid for wholly by the blood of Jesus? Of course it is. Do you still hit the ground? Of course you do. The sin is forgiven but the consequences on this earth are still deadly. The same is true for divorce. The true travesty is that so often the people most affected by the consequences of divorce are the offspring- our children. This is not about us, it is about those who follow us, and we must start taking that into account in everything.

The truth of this understanding can be found in the trends of each passing generation. For instance, today more than ever before, young people often bypass or put off marriage and simply cohabit. Many of them are scared to death of marriage; they want to have a trial run with their partner to make sure they do not end up like the generation before them. Divorce creates doubt and doubt leads to more and more walls being broken down. The same can be said for the current interest in same sex unions or life partners. Young people who have witnessed or even walked through ugly divorces between a man and a woman will often turn to same sex unions as an alternative to the Biblical picture of marriage. The enemy has a way of using the hurt and pain of divorce in one generation to create a fear of the Biblical marriage commitment for the next generation.

We cannot be outwitted by the devil's schemes. We have to deal with the truth of the consequences of our actions for the next generation. (And let me say this to put a stop to all those that would stand in judgment over those who have gone through a divorce. If you think your marriage, your home is not next on the enemy's list, you are sadly mistaken. Satan is good at what he does, which is why you and I must continually ask the God of the universe to protect and prosper our marriages.) If we are going to rebuild the spiritual walls, then we have to be able to understand the areas where the enemy is having his way. This is a big one. **Divorce is one of the leading causes of the spiritual degradation of the next generation in our culture today.**

So guard yourself in your spirit, and do not break faith with the wife of your youth.

Divorce is spiritually crippling our country. The statistics for the divorce rate in America are a bit hard to nail down, but we can fairly say that close to half of all marriages are now ending in divorce. The discipleship machine is broken, and as we have already discussed, it is a trend that could grow with each generation. I am begging you, if you are considering a divorce right now as you are reading this especially if you have children, please ask God to do a miracle in your marriage. Find a Christian counselor to work with; do whatever it takes to see your marriage become all God intends for it to be. We stand with you and encourage you to fight, fight, and then fight some more. I talk with folks all the time who are preparing for divorce, and they tell me they are going to do whatever it takes to fight for their children, but if you really want to fight for your children, fight for your marriage. For those of you who have a great marriage, we also stand with you and encourage you to fight, fight, and keep fighting to honor God in that relationship.

Not too long ago, I was preaching at a youth revival in the Dallas- Fort Worth Area. I was challenging a group of about 300 students to be passionate and driven to overcome some of the travesties that have overtaken our land. I asked them this question, "What do you see in the world today that you really hate? Out of all the injustice the enemy has brought to our land, what would be the one thing you would like to see destroyed?" From the middle of the left side of the room came a small hand that was almost not sticking up high enough for me to see. It was the only hand up.

I called on the young boy, now standing, to share with us what he hated- what he wanted to change in our world. I expected abuse, poverty, world hunger, maybe HIV, but with a beautiful, determined tone in his voice, he simply stated, "Divorce, I want God to put a stop to divorce." My heart broke as the group of students broke into a roaring applause. I was overwhelmed to the point of tears. In each face, I saw the effects of the enemy's devastation. There was not a young person in the room who had not been affected by divorce, and in one accord they agreed with the little hand from the left side of the room- they hate divorce. We have to do whatever it takes to put a stop to the trend of divorce in our nation.

For those of you who have already been through a divorce and especially those of you with children, I want you to listen to me: Hope is not lost. God is bigger than divorce, and He is bigger than the break in the process; He is the process. He stands ready to use you to make strong, life-giving disciples of King Jesus out of your children. He is mighty to save and able above all things to rescue, but we must recognize that divorce has true spiritual consequences for future generations. We cannot ignore that. We must be willing to face divorce, and all that comes with it, head on in the Name of Jesus. When the machine for discipleship is broken, and the spiritual life of a young person hangs in the balance, we must be willing to do whatever it takes to see them trained in righteousness. I said "we" because "we" are the key to seeing the process of discipleship live on even in the midst of brokenness. WE are not defeated. Keep reading- I have some great news to share with you.

Chapter Eight

Alive and Well

Here is where "we" come in. The family is bigger than we think. It has the opportunity to be healthy and thrive even in the midst of the enemy's attacks. One time, as Jesus was teaching in a large crowd, some folks came up to Him and told Him His family was outside. Jesus responded in a really strange way telling the onlookers that His family was not His biological mother and brothers, but His family was anyone who did as His father commanded (Mark 3:32). Did you get that? He is saying that the family truly consists of those who call themselves followers of Jesus. He is saying that the "family" is to be thought of as spiritual not just biological. **The Church is the family of God**, created in the same way to be the perfect mechanism for discipleship. What does that mean today? It means that you and I, the Church of God, must begin to stand in the gap where the spiritual walls are broken. Our call is to be spiritual fathers, mothers, brothers, and sisters to those in need of discipleship. The stakes are high, and the call is great.

> *I looked for a man among them who would build up the wall and stand before me in the gap on behalf of*

*the land so I would not have to destroy it, but I found
none. Ezekiel 22:30*

We are in desperate need of spiritual fathers and mothers
to stand before God in the gap on behalf of the next generation and rebuild the walls. For those of you who do not have
children or your children are adults, you cannot "retire" from
making disciples. This is why the church in America is so
important to the process of rebuilding. We need the wisdom
and life experiences of the older generations of American
Christians to fill the holes left in the walls. For the sake of
the future, we must bridge the gap between our elders and
our infants. For you old-timers out there, let me say this as
an encouragement. I know that the young people of today's
America are a bit weird and often times really loud; but right
now, more than ever before, they need you. They may not be
aware of it yet, but we know you are desperately needed.

They need to get on the roof with you, sit at your feet,
eat your cooking, watch you love your husband, see your
passion for Jesus, and hear the story of how God brought
you from where they are to where you are. It makes my heart
sick that so many of our churches have pushed the elders
of our faith out the door, but take it from a guy with spiky
hair and holes in his jeans, "We need you. Our children need
you. The family cannot function without you. Please hang
in there with us- with our loud music and shorts on Sunday.
The children of tomorrow need the elders of today to disciple
them."

There is a saying in Africa that goes, "It takes a village to
raise a child." And I would contend to say it takes the Church
of God (not the building, but the people) to raise a child in
the Lord. As a family in Christ, we can change the life of
the spiritual Orphas in our cities, churches, and nation. The
Church, the family of God, is the hope of a world in need
of discipleship. This is truly what this book is about for me-

God is calling us, Church, to be The Church for a broken and lost world. We need you- each and every one of you who call yourselves followers of King Jesus- to be family for the next generation. We need spiritual grandmas, spiritual papas, spiritual cousins, aunts, uncles, brothers, sisters, mothers, and most importantly, spiritual fathers.

Never before in human history has the call on the family of God to make disciples been more important than right now, today.

Spiritual Parenting

I wanted to take a special section here to address this issue of spiritual parenting, especially spiritual fathering. In April of 2008, our ministry partnered with the Imagine Network to build and operate a children's orphanage in Kenya, Africa, called the Mattaw Children's Village. Our heart for the orphanage is to rescue the broken and train them to be awesome, life-giving, passionate followers of King Jesus. For the longest time, God has shown me, through His Word, that our call is to rescue the fatherless and care for the widows. In the Old Testament, God accuses Israel of not caring for the fatherless or the widow (Isaiah 1:17-23; Jeremiah 5:28; Psalm 82:3). The New Testament charge in James puts it like this: *Religion that God our Father accepts as pure and faultless is this: to look after orphans and widows in their distress and to keep oneself from being polluted by the world (James 1:26-27).*

Over a period of time and several trips to Africa, God burdened my heart for the fatherless and orphaned children there. But as He began to open my eyes to what He wants to do here for the next generation, I finally made the connection. **The "fatherless" and the "orphaned" are not just children without physical mothers and fathers; they are children without spiritual mothers and fathers.** Wow! Now that certainly changes the landscape of our responsibility and our opportunity. What good would it be if we provided them food to sustain their lives but never gave them the bread of life? God is calling us to spiritually foster the next generation- a generation in desperate need of spiritual parents, especially fathers.

Let me show you the perfect example in the scripture. Look at the language Paul uses in writing to the church at Corinth. *I am not writing this to shame you, but to warn you, as my dear children. Even though you have ten thousand guardians in Christ, you do not have many fathers, **for in Christ Jesus I became your father through the gospel.** Therefore I urge you to imitate me. For this reason I am sending to you **Timothy, my son whom I love**, who is faithful in the Lord. He will remind you of my way of life in Christ Jesus, which agrees with what I teach everywhere in every church (I Corinthians 4:14-17).*

The Apostle Paul is known for being an incredible evangelists and church planter, but Paul's most amazing contribution to the kingdom of God was his understanding and active pursuit of fulfilling "The Great Commission." Look at what he is saying. *You do not have many fathers-* he does not mean physical fathers; he means spiritual fathers. He tells them to imitate him. Why? Because that is what children are supposed to do. They imitate their fathers, as their fathers imitate Jesus, until they can imitate Jesus themselves. He calls Timothy his son- his *spiritual* son. II Timothy 1:5, tells us Timothy inherited his faith from his grandmother and his mother, but according to Acts 16:3, Timothy's father was a Greek, a non-believer. Paul filled the gap in the broken wall of Timothy's life. Timothy needed a spiritual dad, so Paul became that for him.

Timothy is not the only spiritual son Paul adopted. We know Paul also discipled a runaway slave named Onesimus, and Titus, the son of Gentiles. Paul understood what it meant to be a re-builder. He guided these three young men. They went with Paul on several different missionary journeys-they watched him all day everyday, and they imitated him until they came to a point at which they could imitate their true Father in Heaven. All of them became great contributors to the kingdom of God. In a culture where fathers are missing in action both physically and spiritually, the Church has an opportunity to stand in the gap just as Paul did. More certainly, I would contend that each of us who call ourselves disciples of Jesus have a responsibility to do just that.

Let me share a brief story illustrating the awesome power of spiritual parenting. Not too long ago, I was traveling to do a youth retreat with a team of college students serving as group leaders for the weekend. As is our custom, we were doing what I like to call, "My story." The goal is to get each student to share their personal story of life and salvation with the group. The stories are often unbelievable and this day was no different; each story reached another level. When everyone finished telling their story, I came to an eye-opening conclusion; one that reminded me of the truth of our existence and brought me an incredible amount of hope.

I was the only person in the van out of eight people who did not come from a broken home. More than that, several of the young people with me did not even know their biological father or have any relationship at all with their biological mother, but in each story, there was an overwhelming theme connecting them all: Each of them had a neighbor, youth pastor, or even a stepparent who took a spiritual interest in them. The family of God interceded on their behalf and helped disciple them into some of the most beautiful followers of Jesus I have ever met. In return, each of them is on a mission to spiritually foster the next generation.

Just when the enemy thinks he has won, here comes The Church with all the power, authority, and passion of the risen Jesus to stand in the gap on the wall. The Church is the hope of a broken world. One spiritual

orphan at a time, we can rebuild that which the enemy has destroyed. The family of God is not simply a substitute for the biological family; it is far more powerful and capable. Where the earthly family is temporary and broken, the eternal family of God is an unstoppable force the enemy cannot destroy. The family is alive and well.

Chapter Nine

Steel-Toed Boots
(For Men)

My dad worked in the oil fields of West Texas my whole life. Everyday around 4:30 p.m. he came walking in the back door smelling of crude oil. He wore steel-toed boots. I always thought those boots were the coolest things ever until I put them on one day and tried to wear them around. They felt like they weighed fifty pounds each and it became obvious, even to my adolescent brain, that I was not ready to walk around in his shoes even though I always wanted to. I wanted to be like my father, to walk like him, to talk like him, to be strong like him. That is what young boys do- they want to be like the men who lead them, and most often they are. I consider my father to be the single greatest gift the Lord has ever given me (aside from my salvation through Jesus). I know some of you think I am about to be in trouble with my wife and children over that statement, but without my father, I would have never known how to be a husband or a dad.

Redefined "Greatness"

After I graduated from college, I started a career in marketing doing public relations for a large hospital firm. During my first day on the job, I specifically remember sitting behind a large desk in my air-conditioned office, in my suit and tie, when suddenly my father came to mind. Somewhere, at that very moment, he was working in the hot sun trudging through the grime of the West Texas oil fields. I waited until I knew he would be home, and I called the house. When he answered the phone I said, "Hey dad, guess what I am doing? I am pushing a pencil across some paper in my air conditioned office and they are paying me for it." I could hear the tears in my father's voice as he relayed to me how happy he was for me. You see, as a young boy, my father often stated to me that one of the things he wanted for my life, was for me to have an education so I could make a good living pushing a pencil rather than shoveling dirt; he shoveled dirt so I could push a pencil. He sacrificed much of his life to ensure my success. The problem was, like many American men, my definition of "success" was wrong. I missed the lesson that my father tried to teach me my entire life; for a long time, all I could see was "me."

I was after the American Dream. I was determined to go from the trailer house on the wrong side of town to the big house in the right neighborhood. I pledged to myself not to be poor like my family was growing up. I wanted my children to have all the things my father could not give us. I was self-consumed and driven by a need to be "great." I was ambitious and hungry to truly succeed; I wanted to be "somebody." I could not exist in obscurity like my father living in a small town working paycheck to paycheck. It was clear to me in my new world filled with suits and dinner parties that my father was truly a "nobody."

In many ways, even after all he had given me, I became disillusioned by my father's apparent lack of ambition.

I could not understand why he was content to stay where he was living a life without true accomplishment. So one day in my judgmental arrogance, I posed a question to my father about his life's goals. I wanted to know what his ambitions were and what he thought his purpose on Earth was. I wanted to know why he never wanted to be "great." His answer was simple, but it changed my life. With a smile of satisfaction on his face, he told me that his purpose in life, his greatest ambition, was to raise Godly children so they might raise Godly children. I learned later in life that my dad had several offers to make more money or to be the "boss" throughout my years growing up. He turned them all down without a thought because taking them meant he would have to spend more time away from us and that did not fit inside his purpose. There has been much said about the purpose of life by authors and preachers in the last decade, but my father had it right all along.

Men, our purpose on this planet is to make disciples of King Jesus. There exists no higher call, no greater ambition, and no worthier endeavor. In a world where the status of a man is determined by his title, his 401K, his house, and his overall worldly success, my father may be considered a "nobody," but in the Kingdom of God, he is the kind of man God considers "somebody." He is the kind of man we are in desperate need of today. My dad is not perfect, but he taught me more about humility, excellence, kindness, giving, hard work, marriage, responsibility, and following God no matter the cost than all the self-proclaimed "great" men I have ever met. When we were broke, he paid his tithe first; when we were disrespectful to our mother, he disciplined us for mistreating his wife; when we wanted to quit, he showed us how to persevere, and when the world was seemingly falling down around us, he taught us how to stand firm in Jesus.

My father has never preached a sermon, and he is not overly vocal about his faith, but his life is characterized by the fruits of the Spirit of God. My father is one of the "greatest" men I have ever met. My dad will not like being characterized this way because in his humility he understands ultimately he can accomplish nothing without Jesus. In the same way, I understand the impact Jesus has made on me through him. I love you dad, and when I grow up I want to be "great" like you, and my prayer is for my son to feel the same way. You are a man after God's heart, and I am a man after your heart hoping to one day be the kind of man my son can see God in. I want to learn to walk in your boots.

The father is the most important factor in the life of the next generation, and when I say father I want you to think it terms of spiritual fathering (That is inclusive of all Christian men). If you study the statistics for everything from youth suicides to the homeless, from high school dropouts to the staggering numbers of youths in prison, you will find one common theme: the majority of each of those categories is dominated by young people from fatherless homes. There is no way around this truth. Fathers, men, have been the single leading cause of the spiritual brokenness in our country. **Likewise we are the key players in the process of the discipleship of the next generation and rebuilding the spiritual walls of our country.**

Men, we must redefine "greatness" in accordance with God's definition. Men who love their wives selflessly and faithfully are "great" men. Men who father their children with conviction and responsibility are "great" men. Men who defend the spiritually orphaned and the unborn, feed the poor, and cloth the naked are "great" men. Men who can admit their weakness and humble themselves under the awesome God of Heaven are "great" men. Men who live out the Word of God outside the walls of the church building when no one is looking are "great" men. Men who are passionate about their love relationship with Jesus are "great" men. Men who understand there is no greater ambition than to raise Godly children who in turn will raise Godly children are "great" men. By this definition, my father is a great man, and right now in our culture, in our country, we are truly desperate for "great" men. Are you a "great" man?

Take It Like a Man

Because of the emergency we find ourselves in, I need to just say some very straightforward things to our men. I need you to take it like men.

The American man is to be held more accountable than any other single group of people on the planet for the spiritual degradation of our nation.

For too long we have been negligent in making this clear. Men, you and I are the keepers of the spiritual walls that lie in pieces at the feet of the children we have been called to protect. I believe the Lord is sick of the excuses and overall apathy of the American Christian man. We are accountable for what we have created. When we look around at the mess we find ourselves in, we need not look any further than our own arrogance and selfishness for the cause. Yes, satan is at the root of all that is broken, but he only has the ability to destroy what we allow. There is no excuse for the lack of strong spiritual men in our country today and our actions or lack thereof, are unacceptable as a whole. We have spent too much time pursuing our own desires and not enough time caring for and teaching the next generation how to follow Jesus. We need to spend more time shoveling so the next generation can push pencils. If this angers you and causes you to poke your chest out in protest, it is probably because you recognize, just as we all do, that it is true. We cannot ignore it anymore. God designed the man to lead, protect, provide, and be the key piece in the process of discipling the next generation, and we have failed big time. This is not medieval thinking or some legalistic chauvinism; this is the truth of God's intention.

*Now I want you to realize that the head of every man
is Christ, and the head of the woman is man, and the
head of Christ is God. I Corinthians 11:3-4*

God designed everything with order: God, Jesus, man,
woman. Before the women start throwing stuff at me, I want
you to understand this is not about an order of importance or
ability, but it is the order God shows us through His Word.
Does it mean in some messed up religious way that woman
is less than man? No, but what it does mean is that men are
responsible and accountable ultimately under God as leaders.
Let me take you to another picture so we can understand this
accountability together.

According to Romans 5:12-19, Adam, not Eve, is made
accountable for the birth of sin in the garden. As a matter
of fact, the Bible gives us no indication that the effects of
sin actually enter the world until after Adam has eaten the
forbidden fruit, even though Eve beat him to it (Genesis
3:6). When God discovers Adam and Eve have sinned, the
Bible clearly shows God calling Adam into question, as if
He does not know Eve is the one who takes the first bite
(Genesis 3:9). Adam is responsible. The Bible clearly tells
us that Adam is with Eve as she converses with satan and as
she falls prey to his lies (Genesis 3:6). Adam does nothing
to stop her, nothing to protect her, nothing to drive the snake
away from her- he just stands there while the enemy has his
way with his bride. Then, he follows her right into the worst
mistake ever by mankind- sin.

Like our sinful father Adam, many of us as men are guilty
of doing the exact same thing- nothing. While the enemy lies
to our wives and children, we stand by and refuse to move for
fear it may bring unwanted conflict. Be a man for goodness
sake. Rise up in the truth of the scripture of God and punch
the enemy in the mouth. We have not been given a spirit of
fear, but of power, of love, and of self-discipline (II Timothy

1:7). We cannot be timid in our approach to leadership as men- the enemy is certainly not holding anything back.

As we travel across the country to church after church, we see a trend that is hard to miss. Women everywhere are doing an incredible job of taking up the slack for the so-called "Christian men" of our country. I have counseled many women and heard scores of others complain that their husband is not the spiritual leader of their home; I have to disagree. The men are spiritually leading whether we like it or not, often times it is just in the wrong direction. Our absence, apathy, ignorance, and lack of commitment are all directions of spiritual leadership. We are not leading because we are smarter, stronger, or more reliable than our counter-parts; we are leading because that is the position God put us in. For us, leading is not an option, but we have obvious choices to make about the direction in which we lead. It is a disgrace that the women of our country have not only had to hold together our families, but they have also been forced to take on the burden of the church as well.

We are in need of some men who are willing to stand in the gap on the wall and rebuild our homes, our children, and our churches. We need some men with the character of Christ who will love their wives rightly as Jesus himself loved the Church and live up to the responsibility of spiri-tually fathering their children and the spiritual orphans of our country. We need some men who will fight for the next generation of young people and refuse to go quietly into the night while the enemy has his way with our families. So go the men of our country, so will go our country. So go the men in our churches, so will go our churches. If you do not believe me, just look around.

If the Christian men of America do not rescue the next generation from the hand of the enemy, if we do not start leading our nation towards the Lord, no one else will. I have a proposal- either we take the fish off the back of our car, or we start living in a manner worthy of the incredible call God has given us. We have this incredible opportunity as men to change the course of our nation's history, to change the course of our spiritual legacy, and to stand in the gap to rescue the spiritual Orphas who surround us. Regardless of our status or the measure of our worldly success, we have everything we need to be "great" men (2 Peter 1:3-9.)

Mandates of a Great Man

> *Here is a trustworthy saying: If anyone sets his heart on being an overseer, he desires a noble task. Now the overseer must be above reproach, the husband of but one wife, temperate, self-controlled, respectable, hospitable, able to teach, not given to drunkenness, not violent but gentle, not quarrelsome, not a lover of money. He must manage his own family well and see that his children obey him with proper respect.* ***(If anyone does not know how to manage his own family, how can he take care of God's church?)*** *I Timothy 3:1-5*

Don't you find it interesting that when God is giving mandates for Christian leaders in the Church, He judges them based on how they manage their own family? He considers whether or not they are good fathers, good husbands, and men worthy of respect. I do not believe God is saying, "Well if you are not a deacon, or an elder, you can do whatever you want." He is saying that if we want to lead the Church, the next generation of Jesus followers, then we need to start by rightly leading in our own homes. We have too many pompous preachers and so called "great Christian leaders" who put on a good show on Sunday but do not love their wives rightly or care for their children with character and integrity. God cannot honor that kind of leadership. I have felt the sting of this rebuke on far too many occasions having preached a powerful message from the pulpit only to walk off the stage and treat my wife with contempt- there is no greater failure.

Anyone can preach a sermon, as a matter of fact, we have pastors leading churches in America who are not even followers of Christ, but it takes a true man of Godly character to love his wife rightly and rear his children in the Lord. Please do not hear what I am not saying; I am a preacher, and I thank God for the individuals who boldly preach the Word from the pulpit week after week. But we must understand that for us as men, it is not enough to simply exposit well- we must lead well; we must love well. We must make the things that are important to God important to us. We will not be held accountable for how much money we made, what kind of car we drove, or what committees we served on in the church, but for the spiritual legacy we leave our wives and children. Inside the Church, we must stop entrusting men with the spiritual welfare of the next generation based on their public speaking ability, and start appointing men based on their commitment to rightly love and disciple their own families. We need to understand the deeper purpose. **No matter what we have accomplished on this planet as men, if we do not train the next generation in the Lord, we will fail.**

Fathers, do not exasperate your children; instead, bring them up in the training and instruction of the Lord. Ephesians 6:4

When I walk into a room of students in today's world and I tell them that God is our spiritual "father," I often get the strangest looks. For so many students, the word "father" does not bring up good emotions. I consider myself more and more blessed with each passing day because for me the word "father" describes a man who walks out the character of Christ everyday. I also have to be aware that for so many, the words "God" and "father" are complete opposites. I find myself having to paint a detailed picture of how God the Father truly is- which is so different than how many of the next generation sees a "dad."

He is faithful (II Timothy 2:13). He does not lie (I John 5:20). He is love (I John 4:8). He is compassionate (Psalm 103:13). He cares for His children (I Peter 5:7). He protects them (II Thessalonians 3:3). He fights for them (Exodus 14:14). He desires to spend time with them (Matthew 19:14). He loves them without condition (Ephesians 2:4). He disciplines them (Hebrews 12:6). He will never leave them or forsake them (Hebrews 13:5). The children of the next generation, our children, should know these traits of their heavenly Father based on what they see in us; they should know Him based on knowing us, the men of God in the generation before them. No, there is not a man or a father alive who is perfect, but our goal should always be to rightly lead our families and to be holy as God is holy.

There are some additional responsibilities given to men in the Bible. We are called to be the spiritual **pacesetters** for our families, churches, and cities to the Lord (I Corinthians 11:3). We are called to be **providers,** according to I Timothy 5:8, and **protectors** according to Genesis 2:15. Ephesians chapter five tells us that we are to be the kind of **partners** who love our wives as Christ loved the church and gave Himself up for her. Lastly, the Psalmist describes our role as **priest** for our wives and children (Psalm 78). I implore you as men to take a hard, deep look at the responsibilities the Lord has placed on us. If you are not leading in a way worthy of your calling, please ask the Lord to convict your soul and strengthen your spirit for the role He has called us to.

Let me sum up this section with the words from a song written by a band named Jonah 33 (www.jonah33rock.com) called "The Father's Song."

Trying to catch this phenomenon is like trying to capture a flame. Everyone wants to save the world but no one will take the blame. ***And when will we learn the end result of our negligence.*** *Something's wrong, its not quite right. We have misplaced common sense. Excuse me, but has anyone seen everyone's dad, 'cause a boy is the only thing that God can use to make a man. Point the finger at education and we curse the silver screen. The prison system regurgitates and we wonder what does it mean. And boys will be boys but not without a man called dad. Something's wrong, the boy moves on to try to live a life that he's never had, to try to live a life that he'll never have. Look around.* ***The family is a dying breed and broken homes become majority. And the future is always born from example, so where are the men God gave the responsibility to lead?***

If the future is always born from the example set by the men of our country, what will the future of America look like? You and I are the only ones who can decide the answer to that question. We are responsible. In our own lives, we must redefine "greatness" according to the mandates given us by scripture. We must be willing to live out the true call of God on our lives to train the next generation of Jesus followers. We must rearrange our priorities, re-structure our homes and churches, and rally the "great" men of our country for the task of rebuilding the spiritual walls.

If you are a husband, put this book down for a minute and go find your bride. Hug her, kiss her, apologize to her if you need to, and tell her that you are committed to loving her as Jesus loved the church- selflessly. Ask her to pray with and for you, and to stand beside you as you seek to become the "great' man God has called you to be. If you are a father, put down this book and go find your children and hug them like never before. Love on them until they ask what is wrong with you. Then share with them that teaching them how to walk with Jesus is more important to you than your job, your golf game, or even your reputation. Make sure you prove it by making decisions that honor that commitment. Please come right back because if we are ever going to make a change in the spiritual future of our nation, we need every man available.

If you are reading this right now and your heart truly desires to be the kind of man the Lord has called you to be, but you too never had the example you needed, I want to encourage you. Start with the Bible- read it from front to back and over again. Do whatever it takes to align your priorities with those you see laid out in scripture. Call your pastor and share your heart with him. Ask him if there is another man in your church you can follow. There are count-less books, websites, and ministries designed to help you learn how to be a man of God, but nothing will be as good as learning from a Godly man. Whatever you do, please do not just sit there. God wants to mold and shape you into the man He desires then use you to do the same for the coming generations of men.

The Responsible Always Respond

I know we have spent a great deal of time in this section talking about our responsibility, but before we can respond to where we are, we must recognize how we got here to start with. It is imperative that we understand the gravity of our call to bring up the next generation in righteousness. Let me see if I can make one last attempt to convey the seriousness of our responsibility as adults. Listen to the words of Jesus himself in Luke chapter seventeen.

> *Jesus said to His disciples, "Things that cause people to sin are bound to come, but woe to that person through whom they come.* **It would be better for him to be thrown into the sea with a millstone tied around his neck than for him to cause one of these little ones to sin. So watch yourselves.** *Luke 17:1-3*

Jesus is serious about the example we set for the young people of America. He is serious about the things we teach them, the things we plant in them, and about our responsibility to keep them free from sin. "So watch yourselves." Each of us, men and women, parents and pastors, coaches and teachers, big brothers and sisters is responsible and will be held accountable for the discipleship of the next generation.

Before I end this section of the book and get back to Nehemiah, let me say this: In reading the last couple of pages, if you have recognized for the first time that you have dropped the ball when it comes to spiritually leading the next generation, then I need you to know something- **You are not alone**. I have cried many times penning this section of the book because I recognize how I have failed them myself in so many ways. Remember this: The God we serve is bigger than our sin, bigger than our personal fallacy, bigger than our past mistakes, and He is able to save our children and their children beyond our mistakes. This is not about creating shame in our lives over past mistakes; this is about taking the first step to rebuild what the enemy has torn down.

We should never overlook the cleverness or power of satan in this world. His job is to kill, steal, and destroy, and he takes it very seriously. We should too. Do not allow the enemy to use the past to shame you into not changing the future. There is nothing good in us but Jesus. It is because of the love and mercy of God the Father that we have this incredible opportunity to stand together for the sake of our children and their children. Just agree with me before you turn the page that we are going to move forward together under the grace of God and in the authority of King Jesus because the next step to rebuilding is going to push us to the limit.

We will not hide them from their children; **we will**
tell the next generation the praiseworthy deeds of
the LORD, *His power, and the wonders*
He has done. He decreed statutes for Jacob and
established the law in Israel, which He commanded
our forefathers to teach their children,
so the next generation would know them, even the
children yet to be born, and they in turn
would tell their children.
Psalms 78:4-6

Section Four

Respond

Chapter Ten

Don't Change the Channel

I have a confession; I am a late night television watcher. I guess I have a hard time turning my brain off, although some would argue the real problem is I have a hard time turning it on. Nonetheless, I find myself up late at night on many occasions watching Sports Center over and over again, or just flipping channels to distract my mind. For some reason though, no matter how hard I try not to, I always seem to come across that program about the *Feed the Children* ministry. You know the one where they show the little African babies covered in flies and snot, with their bellies poking out from malnutrition, and their skin draped over their little skeletons? Late one night, I was surfing the channels and sure enough I stumbled onto that program. What I did next really took me by surprise; as quickly as I possibly could, I changed the channel. I don't mean I was flipping through and just moved on to something else; it was deliberate and quick. It was as if I was afraid of what was there.

It was not too long until my Spirit posed some questions to me. "Why did you do that Kevin? Why did you change the channel so fast? Why are you avoiding this program? Is that how the Lord has called you to respond to the reality of the brokenness in our world?" I was convicted and thought,

"Come on Lord, I am trying to turn my mind off. I am trying to have some "me" time. I don't want to mess with this right now." I reluctantly turned the channel back to the program, hoping it was over, but as the Spirit would have it, I caught it just as it was restarting. For the first time, I watched it in its entirety. Tears began pouring down my face. With every story, every little face, I just kept watching and listening until my heart was completely broken- broken enough for me to respond. Every time I see the program now, I stop and watch for a while- at least long enough for my heart to break once again. I find that I am slowly learning why.

We have talked much about our responsibility and the overwhelming devastation that has occurred in our nation due to our negligence, but our response to this understanding is paramount to being part of the solution. I want to remind you of the response of Nehemiah to hearing the news that the city of God and people of God are broken down.

When I heard these things, I sat down and wept. For some days, I mourned and fasted and prayed before the God of Heaven. Nehemiah 1:4

Nehemiah responds to the reality of the brokenness of his people in the most incredible way. He is not in denial about the situation, and unlike me, he does not quickly reach for the remote. He just sits there and breaks in half. He is beside himself with grief, and his actions speak to the seriousness of his concern. Nehemiah is teaching us an incredible lesson about how God desires us to respond to the truth of our current reality. Nehemiah is broken.

Brokenness has a way of changing our perspective, a way of challenging our hearts beyond our own complacency. It digs deep to remove the layers of our calloused hearts and creates a sense of urgency and desperation. Brokenness purifies our motivations and draws us close to the heart of

God. Time and again in the years leading up to Nehemiah's response, God pleads for His people to come to Him in brokenness. He pleads for them to put down the remote and allow the reality of their sin and the devastating results of that sin to penetrate their hardened hearts.

Brokenness Gets God's Attention

For so long in our country, when faced with the reality of the spiritual degradation of the future generations, we too have been guilty of changing the channel. Just like I did that night, we have responded by trying to ignore it or pretend it does not exist. We have responded selfishly and arrogantly. "I don't want to talk about those things because they hurt my feelings." "If we just think more positively, then things will change." "It's too overwhelming to think about, so I just try not to." "Well, we can't save them all." On and on it goes, excuse after excuse and nothing changes. Instead, we just watch the channels that do not challenge the way we live until our minds are numb once again and we are lulled back to sleep.

Nehemiah is instantly broken; he is ruined and refuses to shut his eyes to the pain of his people. He is not concerned about whether or not this news hurts his feeling. Of course it does; it should hurt all of our feelings. No human alive especially those who claim to follow the merciful and loving God of the Bible should be able to recognize the devastation and just change the channel. I have rationalized myself into doing nothing on an everyday basis, but the truth is that I do not want my self-consumed life to be interrupted by the call of God. It cost me too much to care. It is too messy. Brokenness is a huge threat to our selfishness and the overall comfort of our everyday existence, so our response is quite simple: we just change the channel.

Our first response to the issues facing our nation and our children should be a broken heart- broken beyond repair. Yes, the truth of the situation is ugly. Yes, it is overwhelming, but we must understand that nothing will ever change until we allow the truth to penetrate the deepest parts of who we are. Until we are so broken-hearted that we cannot sit by and watch the enemy destroy family after family, we will not act. I want you to do a little exercise with me in the coming days. Go down to your local mall or anywhere young people or children hang out. Pray for God to break your heart over what breaks His heart. Ask Him to open your eyes to the truth of the pain of our children. I want you to sit there, watch, and listen until your heart begins to ache and you cannot hold back the tears. Stay there until your heart is inspired to act.

This is the place where we discover our breakthrough, where we begin to truly find the inspiration needed to go the distance in the marathon for the souls of our children. This is where we gain the ear of the God whose very nature is to rescue. True brokenness gets the attention of God. King David knows this and writes, *"The LORD is close to the brokenhearted and saves those who are crushed in spirit" (Psalm 34)*. He knows all about being brokenhearted and crushed in Spirit. Isaiah makes a similar proclamation in one of my favorite pieces of scripture in the entire Bible. Isaiah sixty-one describes the very purpose for which Jesus came to this Earth:

> *The Spirit of the Sovereign LORD is on me, because the LORD has anointed me to preach good news to the poor.* ***He has sent me to bind up the broken- hearted,*** *to proclaim freedom for the captives and release from darkness for the prisoners, to proclaim the year of the Lord's favor and the day of vengeance of our God, to comfort all who mourn, and provide for those who grieve in Zion—to bestow on them a crown of beauty instead of ashes, the oil of gladness instead of mourning, and a garment of praise instead*

of a spirit of despair. They will be called oaks of righ-teousness, a planting of the LORD for the display of His splendor. Isaiah 61:1-3

Some seven hundred years after this prophecy by Isaiah, Jesus walks into church one day, picks up the scroll of the prophet Isaiah, and reads the first few lines of this text. He then rolls the scroll back up, gives it to the scroll holder guy, and says, "This scripture is fulfilled in your hearing" (Luke 4:20). He is saying, "This is about me. I came into the world to bind up the brokenhearted." Throughout the gospels, Jesus is found declaring that He came into the world for the thirsty, the sick, the lame- He came for the broken. God sent His son to fix our brokenness. He hears the cries of the desperate and destitute, but if we continue to change the channel on our reality and choose not to allow our situation to break us, then we cannot expect God to move on our behalf. It is not the healthy who need a doctor; it is the sick (Matt. 9:12). We are sick, and our healer is standing in our midst. Nehemiah gains the ear of God because he is broken over the exact things that break the heart of God. If you and I have the heart of God, we too should respond this way.

All Worked Up

When I speak this message to people, there are always a couple of aristocrats who come up to me and say, "Well Kevin, you don't expect us to walk around all day in despair do you?" No, this is not about despair. The God we serve is not a God of despair and He is still on the throne, but there must be a point where we decide that we care enough to be a part of the solution. This kind of brokenness breeds passion and destroys the complacency that has set itself up in our hearts. This is about the heart of God. Look at this scripture with me out of the book of Amos.

Woe to you who are complacent in Zion, and to you who feel secure on Mount Samaria, you notable men of the foremost nation, to whom the people of Israel come! Go to Calneh and look at it; go from there to great Hamath, and then go down to Gath in Philistia. Are they better off than your two kingdoms? Is their land larger than yours? You put off the evil day and bring near a reign of terror. You lie on beds inlaid with ivory and lounge on your couches. You dine on choice lambs and fattened calves. You strum away on your harps like David and improvise on musical instruments. You drink wine by the bowlful and use the finest lotions, but you do not grieve over the ruin of Joseph. Therefore you will be among the first to go into exile; your feasting and lounging will end. Amos 6:1-7

Is it just me or does this sound like us? What God has against these people is not that they use the finest lotions, but that their hearts are not broken over the sin of their nation. They change the channel to keep the reality of their people from messing up their complacent lives. Complacency is the result of comfort. When you allow God to really get a hold of you, when you allow Him to break your heart over what breaks His heart, it is not comfortable and you cannot be complacent. Does your heart break for the travesties of the coming generations in America, or are you reaching for the remote right now?

Let me share a story with you that happened not too long after I started in the ministry-something I will never forget. After preaching a message in church one day, one of the pastors came up to me and said, "Well, that sure was spunky. I really appreciate your passion for that subject, but you need to realize not everyone thinks like you. When you have been in the ministry long enough to understand a little better how things normally go, you won't get so worked up over this stuff." I almost lost it. I was doing my very best, but it was no use. I yelled through my clinched teeth, "If staying in the ministry for as long as you have will make me like you, I will quit tomorrow." I know I should have kept my mouth closed, but this pessimistic attitude is at the core of our complacency.

Is the God we serve not a consuming fire? Did He not brutally sacrifice His only son for our pathetic selves? Is hell less hot or have the rules of eternity changed so you can just get into Heaven by popular vote? Did Jesus himself not come to the Earth to bind up the brokenhearted, to set the captives free, and then leave us the Holy Spirit so we can continue His work? If you hold any position in ministry and do not get "worked up" over issues of sin, the power of the cross, the undeniable love of the Lord, or the brokenness of our children, please quit. At least find a way to come before the Lord honestly until your heart once again beats like God's heart.

We need to rid our church leadership of anyone whose heart does not pound out of their chest over the sin destroying our world. We do not need another well thought out sermon from a guy who is moving up the corporate church ladder; we need to identify those whose hearts burn for the broken and who have a deep, passionate relationship with the King. We need to stop putting people in leadership roles based on their education or their outstanding resume, and start letting those broken over the "ruin of Joseph" lead the charge. These are the kinds of leaders who have the attention and support of God.

As you can see, I get a bit "worked up," but I cannot apologize for it. It is the same passion that stirs Nehemiah. His brokenness drives him to respond in the right way- one that honors a God who takes very seriously the plight of the destitute. As we travel from church to church and share this message, I find too many Christian leaders who are not "worked up" about anything. I want to encourage those of you today who are knee-deep in the brokenness of the next generation: school teachers, pastors, nurses, coaches, social workers, ministers or parents- I know it is difficult and there are many days when you feel like giving up, but you must trust that the investments you are making today will pay eternal dividends. Although you may not see the fruit of your tireless labor today, God is faithful to bring the increase. He will honor your brokenness over the "ruin of Joseph."

I have been told repeatedly that I should protect myself and not expect too much to change so my heart will not get broken over and over again. That kind of thinking is nothing more than a lie from the enemy himself. He has convinced us the task is too large, the sacrifice is too great, and the results are not worth the effort. The devil is a liar. He tries these exact tactics with Jesus when he tempts Him in the desert (Luke 4:1-13). During this temptation, Jesus knows there is incredible heartbreak ahead. He knows the pain and sacrifice will be great. He knows the task seems impossible, but He refuses to allow sin and death to win. He refuses because He is certain the results are worth it. I am forever grateful that He accepts the pain, the heartache, and the death my sin brought Him. I am grateful that He got all "worked up" over me.

God built you and me to be the dwelling place of His Spirit. The same spirit that raised Christ from the dead lives in those of us who have a relationship with Jesus. He calls us by His name and charges us to save the world with the gospel of Jesus. He gives us the ministry of reconciliation (II Corinthians 5:19) and declares that we can do more than we could ever think or imagine according to the power that is at work in us (Ephesians 3:20). Complacency has no place in the ministry of the gospel of Jesus, and we must lead the charge in breaking up the fallow ground. When we recognize the state of emergency we are in, it will give us a sense of urgency, desperation, and a brokenness that will push us beyond our apathy. In speaking about the End Times, Jesus makes this statement in Matthew 24:12, *"Because of the increase of wickedness the love of most will grow cold, but he who stands firm to the end will be saved."* As the wickedness increases in our world, we must not lose the faith or the fervor God calls us to walk in; we cannot afford to grow cold. God calls us to move with passion and zeal unmatched by the enemy. Only then, will our hearts will be alive with the hope that is Jesus.

Chapter Eleven

Love Sick

I want to let you in on why my heart beats so passionately about Nehemiah's response and about our need to follow his example. One day while serving as a youth pastor, I was sitting in my office thinking about some of the things I needed to accomplish that day when my gorgeous wife walked in. I have no idea where the question came from, but I turned to my wife and asked her very simply, "Kimberly, when was the last time you remember seeing me brokenhearted over one of our students? I mean when was the last time you saw me just weep over someone who is lost or hurting?" Kim was evidently pretty involved in something else because she did not even look at me when she answered, "I don't know Kev- I would have to think about it." My mind began to race. Searching my memory for a moment of brokenness, I could not identify even one in the recent past.

That afternoon, God took me to a scripture that has become a life verse for me. It is found in II Corinthians 5:14 and simply says, *"For the love of Christ compels us."* I sat with the Lord for a long time that day asking myself these questions, "Does the love of Christ compel me, or am I motivated by a selfish desire to be known by man? Is my pursuit of more students about advancing Your Kingdom or just about being bigger than the church across town? Am I truly passionate about God's glory or has ministry just become an obligation to me?" It did not take long to learn the answers. Not too much time passed before I lost what had become my "job," and I set out on a journey toward brokenness.

I am not a scholar by any means, but over the years, I have had the chance to study this verse in more detail. I discovered that the word "compels" has several meanings. As a matter of fact, the KJV and the NASB translations of the Bible both translate it differently than the NIV. The word means to constrain, control, or afflict. I fell in love with the last one- for the love of Christ "afflicts" us. In effect, it makes us lovesick. I don't know about you, but my love for my wife has made me do some really out of character things. If you have ever been lovesick you know exactly what I am talking about. When you are lovesick, you are straight-up out of your mind. You will change the way you dress, talk, eat, and stay up really late talking on the phone about nothing. It is a spell of some kind that does not come off with soap. Your heart is captured, your mind is consumed, and you would run around the world, or walk through fire for that love. Now, just think about what you would do if you were compelled by the love of the Lord- Maybe hang on a cross to save those torturing you?

There is an analogy I often share when talking about this exact subject, so if you hear me preach and I share this story, please act like you have never heard it before. **This story is not true,** but I want to share it from the first person perspective so it will make more sense. One night I woke up and smelled smoke in my house. I sat up in bed to notice my wife and little girl in bed with me. (My wife was there because she is my wife, and my daughter was there because she has a supernatural ability to float through walls in the middle of the night and land in my bed.) I quickly got up and went to the door leading from my bedroom to the living room. When

I opened the door, my living room was engulfed in flames. I got the girls out of bed and went out the bedroom window.

When I got into the front yard, the fire department was already there along with the National Guard, Navy Seals, and Army Rangers. They all greeted us and told us how glad they were that we all got out safely. They informed us that the house was engulfed in flames and no one would be allowed to go back in for any reason. What they did not know was that my son was asleep in the back bedroom.

Let me ask you a question right here. Is there a National Guard, Navy Seal, or Army Ranger who could keep you from going back into that house to save your child? If you are a parent, you know the answer is "No." There is not an army on the planet that could keep me from going back into that house, but why? Am I running back in because I am obligated to or because it is my job as a dad? Is it because I want to be a hero or feel guilty for getting out alive? No, I am running back into the burning house because love is compelling me beyond the flames, beyond the fear, beyond the pain, and beyond myself.

When we allow the Lord to break us and compel us by His love, we are willing to do whatever it takes to see our children rescued. This is the kind of passion that should consume us in our relationship with the Lord. It fuels the desire to see the broken healed and lost ones saved.

For God so what? For God so loved the world that He sent His Son (John 3:16). Romans 5:8 declares that "God demonstrates His own love for us in this: While we were still sinners Christ died for us." The cross is a demonstration of God's love for us. What is our demonstration of love for those following us? The Bible tells us God Himself is Love and His greatest desires for us are to love Him with everything we have and love others as ourselves (Matthew 22:37-40). It is love, not obligation or some messed up religious points system that brings us to our knees and causes us to surrender. Love makes the world go round; it is the force that causes us to obey God (John 14:15) and to run recklessly into a thirsty world with a drink of water, into a lost generation with the truth of Jesus.

Love rearranges our priorities and keeps us up late at night. It brings us to our knees and makes us angry. It pushes us beyond our complacency. It makes us sick. It afflicts us to the point where we cannot standby and watch the next generation spiritually die. God's love is selfless not proud. It always protects, hopes, and perseveres. It covers a multitude of sins. It never fails. The love of the Lord in our own lives is truly the root of our passion, and the pure motivation needed to be repairers of the broken walls. This time around, we cannot afford to fail. Unless we are motivated by the love of the Lord, we will.

The love given us by the God of the universe will bring compassion for those around us and push us beyond ourselves. The Passion of the Christ is not just a movie; it is an example of the way you and I are to love the world. I have seen grown men paint their chest and stand in freezing rain to cheer on eleven guys in tights at a football game. They get in fistfights defending their team. They love their team and it shows. It is ridiculous, but the fruit of their passion is obvious. As the love of God compels us, we will be willing to make fools of ourselves in freezing rain and fight to defend our families, the widow, the defenseless, the unborn, and the orphaned. This is the heart of God. When was the last time you were broken to the point of tears over the sin of our world or the devastation of the coming generation? Truly, take a moment to answer that question. Has our response been as Nehemiah's response?

Too Sick to Eat?

Nehemiah sat down and wept for days, but then he allowed his brokenness and passion to push him to another level. He not only wept and mourned, but he fasted and prayed for days. Have you ever been too sick to eat? How serious are we about seeing God rescue the children of the next generation? Are we willing to stop eating for days? It seems extreme, but *fasting can be described as a denial of our physical bodies in order to obtain a spiritual breakthrough.* Fasting is not punishment or penance; it is, however, one of the most powerful tools we have as children of God for calling God's attention to the seriousness of our situation.

When teaching about fasting in Matthew chapter six, Jesus does not say, "If you fast," He says, "When you fast," implying that we are to use fasting as a discipline in our walk with Him. In the Old Testament, we see some incredible pictures of how God honors the collective fasting of His people with overwhelming victories in battle and by staying His hand of judgment. One of my favorite scriptures on the declaration of a fast designed to gain the attention and mercy of the Lord is found in Joel chapter two. Joel is writing the people of Israel about the devastation they have endured and about the seriousness of their impending future. In the midst of his rebuke, he passionately implores the people of God to declare a holy fast before the Lord. In essence, he gives them a huge key to reviving the nation of God. He gives them some much needed instructions for rebuilding. Listen to the tone and the heart of his message to them:

"Even now," declares the LORD, "return to me with all your heart, with fasting and weeping and mourning. Rend your heart and not your garments. Return to the LORD your God, for He is gracious and compassionate, slow to anger and abounding in love, and He relents from sending calamity. Who knows? He may turn and have pity and leave behind a blessing- grain offerings and drink offerings for the LORD your God. Blow the trumpet in Zion, declare a

__holy fast, call a sacred assembly__. Gather the people, consecrate the assembly; bring together the elders, gather the children, those nursing at the breast. Let the bridegroom leave his room and the bride her chamber. Let the priests, who minister before the LORD, weep between the temple porch and the altar. Let them say, 'Spare your people, O LORD. Do not make your inheritance an object of scorn, a byword among the nations.' Why should they say among the peoples, 'Where is their God?' Then the LORD will be jealous for His land and take pity on His people." Joel 2:12-18

Joel instructs them to declare a holy fast and rend their hearts not just their garments. He is saying let your hearts break; let your souls grieve rather than just fulfilling some religious duty by outwardly tearing your clothes. The ripping of garments in the Bible is a sign of a repentant heart, but God is not fooled by religious acts alone. **Fasting is not something we do based on religious obligation; it is birthed out of a heart that is desperate for the Lord- a heart that is broken to the point at which it desires His spiritual intercession more than our earthly concession.**

Did you notice the sense of urgency Joel implores them with? He says, "Let the bridegroom leave his room and the bride her chamber." Joel recognizes the emergency; similarly, we must put everything on hold until we come broken and honestly before the Lord. Why? Simply put, there is nothing more important than reaching the next generation with Jesus. The question for us is, "How important is this call on our lives? How important is it to you that your children, your neighbor's children, and the children of America walk with Jesus? Is it important enough for us to fast, humble ourselves, pray, and seek God daily?" This is about doing the hard things.

Throughout the Old and New Testament, we see Biblical mandates for God's people to fast. In Exodus 34:28, Moses fasts for forty days upon receiving the Ten Commandments and in intercession for the people of Israel who provoke God by worshipping a golden calf in his absence. Samuel fasts to intercede for the Israelites when the Philistines are preparing to crush them (I Samuel 7:5-9). Ezra declares a fast for the entire group of Jews returning to Jerusalem after the exile asking God for protection from the enemy (Ezra 4:16). Esther asks the Jews in Susa to fast to intercede for her before she goes to King Xerxes knowing that she could be killed for defending the people of God (Esther 4:16). Jesus himself fasts in the desert for forty days as He withstands the temptations of satan before He begins His public ministry (Luke 4).

It is obvious that fasting is a key component in drawing the attention of God to our brokenness and seeing Him move on our behalf. So why don't we do it? I would say the majority of the people in our country who call themselves Christians have never fasted from anything for any reason. More importantly, and even more devastating, our churches are not fasting as a congregational act of worship or teaching the importance of fasting. We must get back to the basics of our faith. If we truly desire to see God do the miraculous in rebuilding our homes, cities, and nation, we must be willing to honor Him in the ways He has instructed. Fasting is hard, uncomfortable, and physically and emotionally draining, but spiritually, it is a door leading to the miraculous. We need the miraculous. (There are many books on fasting much better than anything I can share with you, and I encourage you to pick one up before you fast if you have not done it before.)

Do Something- Pray

Nehemiah fasts, mourns, weeps, and prays for days. As a matter of fact, Nehemiah prays for four months after hearing of the devastation before he goes to the king to request permission to go to Jerusalem and start physically rebuilding the walls. Although he does not lift a stone to start physically rebuilding the walls for quite some time, Nehemiah starts rebuilding the walls the moment he starts praying to the Lord. Here is what I want to us to know:

Prayer is not what we do before we do something, prayer is doing something.

For the longest time, I looked at prayer as a question and answer session with the Lord. "O.K. God I am praying about what to do about this situation or that situation." And yes, prayer is ultimately where we discover the next direction that God intends for us to go, but it is so much more than that. For so long, we have simply considered prayer the preamble before an event designed to bring restoration to the broken and sight to the blind, but we have it completely backwards. Prayer is the event that brings about restoration and salvation. One of the greatest prayer warriors of the last century, Edward Bounds, puts it this way: *Prayer is the greatest of all forces, because it honors God and brings Him into active aide[12].*

When we pray, we involve the only true source of revival and restoration- the God of Heaven and Earth. God does not need us to accomplish anything, but it should be our great pleasure to live out His call on our lives (Acts 17:24-25). When we begin to petition God in prayer, we call on the authority and power given us by the blood of Jesus and the empty tomb. Prayer changes things, and I truly believe there are many men and women living out the call of God on their lives today because of the faithful prayers of a mother or a grandmother.

I am convinced that my mother has a direct line to God. She has a DSL or high-speed connection while I still have dial up. When she gets together with the women of my tiny home church and they pray- things happen. Now is she out there on the front lines doing youth work or working in a day care with the next generation? No, but she is on the front lines of the war being fought in the heavens for the souls of the next generation. She is petitioning the only God who can save to do exactly that. She understands that "our struggle is not against flesh and blood, but against the rulers, against the authorities, against the powers of this dark world and against the spiritual forces of evil in the heavenly realms" (Ephesians 6:12). Prayer is our first line of defense against the powers of the demonic forces of the universe.

The fervent prayer of the righteous is the most effective tool in protecting and rebuilding the spiritual walls of the next generation. James 5:16 tells us that, *"The prayer of a righteous man is powerful and effective."* Prayer succeeds when all else fails. Prayer is powerful, and unlike so many of the things we put our hope in, it is effective. Jim Cymbala, the pastor of the Brooklyn Tabernacle, has experienced first hand the power of faithful prayer and contends that, **"Only turning God's house into a house of fervent prayer will reverse the power of evil so evident in the world today.**[13]**"** This is where we truly fight the battle raging for the souls of the next generation. We call on God to defend them, rescue them, save them, empower them, and to give us the strength, wisdom, power, and passion to be His hands and feet in the process of rebuilding. We must pray. We need to start yesterday.

Over the course of the past ten years, I have been to what seems like hundreds of deacons meetings, church business meetings, and staff meetings where we prayed about everything from the color of the carpet in the sanctuary to how many services we should have on Easter, but I have been to very few prayer meetings where the central focus for the meeting was to pray for the discipleship of the next generation. I have been to very few prayer meetings called solely to pray for the souls of our children and their children. I have been to very few prayer meetings where we prayed that God would rescue the marriages of American families, rebuild the spiritual walls around our children, or inspire our men to lead us rightly. I am not saying these kinds of prayer meetings do not exist, but I know they do not exist enough. If we want to rebuild the spiritual walls for our children and their children, we must pray.

Section Five

Remember and Repent

Chapter Twelve

Forgotten God

Like Nehemiah, we recognize the brokenness, see clearly our responsibility to the process of rebuilding, and are compelled by the love and passion of the Lord to rebuild, but how? Where do we start? Nehemiah shows us the first steps to our restoration by modeling fervent prayer and even fasting, but I want you to see what he prays and how he prays it. His response combines all the essential elements to invoking the power of the Lord for our rebuilding effort.

Look at the first part of it with me:

"O LORD, God of Heaven, the great and awesome God, who keeps His covenant of love with those who love Him and obey His commands. . ." Nehemiah 1:5

Wow, this is so good! Look at how Nehemiah approaches the Lord: in humility and with a true understanding of God's promise and His glory. Nehemiah starts by rightly exalting the name of the Lord and declares Him to be the great and awesome God. The God we serve is the great and awesome God, the maker of Heaven and Earth, the author of life, the beginning and the end. He is the God who supernaturally rescued His people out of the hands of Pharaoh. He crushed the mighty Goliath with a single stone from the hand of a shepherd boy named David. He is the God who rescued Jonah from the sea, Daniel from the lion's den, and three young Jewish boys named Shadrach, Meshach, and Abednego from the fire. He alone is the God who sits enthroned in the heavens and declares Himself mighty to save. He is the God who sacrificed His only son, so you and I could be whole, forgiven, healed, and restored. *He is the God who keeps His covenant of love with those who love Him and obey His commands.*

This is the where everything changes. Though the enemy is at large, though the task of rebuilding the spiritual walls of our country seems overwhelming, we serve the great and awesome God who stands ready to intercede on our behalf and on behalf of the coming generations. I want to remind those of you wading through the brokenness of our children everyday to *remember the promises of God*: He is big enough. He is patient and just. He is faithful and merciful. He is loving and strong. He is unmatched by the weapons of the enemy. Yes, God can restore your marriage and bring healing to your soul and the souls of your children; He can still change the heart of your wayward son. He can restore your wife's faith in you. He can erase the mistakes of yesterday, and He can rebuild the spiritual walls our children so desperately need. He has not abandoned us or turned a deaf ear. He is merciful and full of grace, but like Nehemiah we must be willing to acknowledge His sovereignty.

We must remember God. Look at the warning God gives the ancestors of Nehemiah before He blessed them with the abundance of Canaan:

> **When you have eaten and are satisfied,** *praise the* **LORD** *your God for the good land He has given you.* **Be careful that you do not forget the LORD**

*your God, failing to observe His commands, His laws and His decrees that I am giving you this day. Otherwise, when you eat and are satisfied, when you build fine houses and settle down, and when your herds and flocks grow large and your silver and gold increase and all you have is multiplied, **then your heart will become proud and you will forget the LORD your God,** who brought you out of Egypt, out of the land of slavery. He led you through the vast and dreadful desert, that thirsty and waterless land, with its venomous snakes and scorpions. He brought you water out of hard rock. He gave you manna to eat in the desert, something your fathers had never known, to humble and to test you so that in the end it might go well with you. **You may say to yourself, "My power and the strength of my hands have produced this wealth for me." But remember the LORD your God, for it is He who gives you the ability to produce wealth,** and so confirms His covenant, which He swore to your forefathers, as it is today. Deuteronomy 8:10-18*

God instructs His people not to forget that He alone saved them from the hand of Pharaoh, and He alone is able to provide for them. He warns them not to become proud or arrogant and presume that they brought themselves great wealth by their own power. God gives them this instruction before they enter the land, but they do not heed His warning and eventually end up in captivity- their walls are broken by their own negligence. Look at this scripture in Hosea 13:4-6 detailing what happens after they inherit the Promise Land.

But I am the LORD your God, who brought you out of Egypt. You shall acknowledge no God but me, no Savior except me. I cared for you in the desert, in *the land of burning heat. When I fed them, **they were** **satisfied; when they were satisfied, they became** **proud; then they forgot me.***

He fed them and they were satisfied, and when they were satisfied, they became proud and forgot God. Sound familiar? Welcome to America, the land of plenty, and the home of the proud. There it is in black and white. It grieves my heart knowing that after all God has done for our nation, we are wasting away in our own arrogance. Remember we are a nation whose motto is, "One nation under God." We must remember that He alone is God, not us. The spiritual brokenness of our nation is simple- it is the result of having forgotten God. The overwhelming evil residing in the hearts of our people is simply the absence of God. This is one of the enemy's oldest and most effective tricks- convincing us we no longer need God.

The hearts of men are only wicked all the time. It is in our very nature that we continually desire to steal the glory of the Lord. This is the danger of living in the land of plenty. Before long, we begin to assume we have accomplished much in our own strength and find ourselves relying on the provision and not the Provider. We have become complacent and self-reliant. We are quick to forget that our abundance is the work of God, not us. We are fat with the provision of the world. Like Sodom, we are, *"**arrogant**, overfed, and uncon-cerned; [we] do not help the poor and needy (Ezekiel 16:49).* Our abundance has made us spiritually lazy. We think we are no longer desperate for the intercession of the Lord, but we are mistaken. The greatness of our nation is contingent upon our reliance on a holy God; without that, we are no different than the world we so quickly judge.

The people of Israel are enslaved to Pharaoh for 400 years. The Bible tells us it is God who hears their desperate cries, and He alone rescues them when they cannot rescue themselves. He brings them into a land of "freedom." Like Israel, we have fallen into the trap of a "land flowing with milk and honey." Our so-called "freedom" has produced for us the gravest kinds of spiritual slavery. Our forefathers understood that God gives us freedom to escape sin and have victory over its bondage, but we have used our freedom as an excuse to do whatever we please-to sin.

We abort our babies and call it "freedom of choice." We allow for every kind of sexual immorality and call it "freedom of sexual preference." We divorce one another at record numbers and call it the "pursuit of happiness." We refuse to hold our leaders accountable for their actions because we fear it may intrude on their "personal liberties." We curse God and deny His existence and call it "freedom of religion." God gives us freedom but we have to be careful not to *"turn your freedom into an opportunity for the flesh"* (Galatians 5:13). Our "success" has caused us to rely on our own abilities and wealth. Our prosperity has caused us to become increasingly selfish and stolen our sense of urgency and desperation. Our self-declared "independence" has deceived us into believing we do not have to be dependant on a Holy God.

What we need more than anything at this point in our history is to make a new declaration- we need to make a "Declaration of Dependence" on a Holy God. We have become slaves of our own devices, and unless God does something miraculous to rebuild the walls, our future generations are going to pay an even greater price.

We need God in our families, in our churches, in our government, and in our lives. Every time a wake up call sounds in our nation, we recognize and remember God for a brief moment, but our arrogance soon leads us to puff ourselves up with the notion that we are a strong people, and we can rebuild. I will never forget one of the first speeches I heard after the tragedy at Virginia Tech; the entire speech was about how strong, smart, and resilient we are. In it, the speaker promised we would move beyond the terror in our own strength. I know she was trying to provide some hope and encouragement in the midst of the overwhelming brokenness, but *our* strength, *our* power, *our* righteousness is no hope at all; it is a false hope that will soon be dashed by the next tragedy.

I cried many tears over that sentiment because my heart cried out to say to those who are hurting and broken, "Remember God- He is the great and awesome God, who has overcome sin and death through His son Jesus. He loves you, and unlike the promise makers of the world, He is faithful even beyond the grave. Our hope has to be in Him, not in our own strength. Let us remember Him." Listen to me, if we truly desire to see the spiritual walls of our nation strong again, we must recognize that we are small, weak, and in need of a Holy God-we are a people DEPENDENT on God. We must remember God!

Chapter Thirteen

Jesus, Jesus, Jesus...

I want to share a story about my own arrogance and the lesson God continues to teach me about our true need for Him. Five or six years ago, I was doing some work with a mission team in South Africa. One morning, the ministry informed us we would be going to a refugee village where many of the people were dying of HIV/AIDS. I remember thinking on the dusty bus ride out there how this was going to make for a great blog or story for the newsletter. "Kevin Kirkland, the great white preacher from America, brings comfort to the dying people of South Africa." God was about to make me small. A pastor friend of mine and I climbed off the bus and starting walking from house to house. We soon had quite a large following of children. One of the young boys following us was named Simon. I asked him to take us to the homes of people who were dying of "the disease." (Little did I know I would be visiting almost every hut.)

As we approached a particular hut, I asked Simon to tell me the situation of the family there. He informed me that the father, aunt, and grandmother had recently died, and the mother was very sick. We walked into this one room hut and found the mother lying motionless and cold on the floor. She was not dead, but she was headed there quickly.

We prayed for her and walked out of the hut to find two young boys standing there. They were the only two children of the woman inside. They lost their entire family and were moments away from losing their mother. I stopped to pray for them, but you will not believe what I did next.

I got down on the ground in my seventy dollar jeans and put my hands on the dirty, snotty, diseased-filled face of this six year old boy. (Because of malnutrition, he was about the size of a four year old in the States.) I pulled him close to me and began to pray. The problem was, surprisingly, no words were coming out of my mouth- I could not speak. My mind and my mouth were completely mute. Out of all the eloquent prayers I have prayed, of the countless scriptures I have memorized, of all the worship songs I know, of all the sermons I have preached, I could not utter a word- God was about to teach me something I will never forget. My mind began to race; my heart began to break. I was fighting to come up with words adequate enough to say over this young boy. There were none.

What could I say? This little boy is probably going to lose his only caregiver in a matter of hours, days at best. I had nothing. I could not muster a word. I just sat there in the dirt and cried. The great white preacher from America had nothing to offer this little boy. And then. . . a word. One single word began to quietly creep through my lips. JESUS. JESUS. JESUS. . . It was the only word I could speak. I just spoke it over and over again, and with each repetition, I began to gain some clarity. This young boy needed Jesus. I need Jesus. My son and daughter need Jesus. The children of America need Jesus. Our marriages, our homes, our churches, our government, our nation, all need Jesus. Nothing else will do.

Can you see it? Without Jesus, what can we truly offer the broken and beaten? Unless the Lord builds the house, we labor in vain- unless the Lord rebuilds the next generation, we labor in vain (Psalm 127:1). This little boy did not need my podcast or a three point sermon and a poem. My "higher education" was of no use, and my personal wealth could not truly change his situation. He did not need my autograph or my latest devotional book. He did not need the "great white preacher from America." He could not care less about the building campaign at my "church," the new children's program, or the size of the crowd on Sunday morning- none of those things could save him. He was dying, his world was crashing in around him, and neither my American religion nor my status in the corporate American church could change that for a single second. He needed Jesus, and nothing else would do.

It is the same today as it has always been: restoration, revival, and regeneration are all about Jesus. Jesus is the Savior. Jesus is the hero who came down out of Heaven to take on the sins of the world and the evil forces of the enemy, defeating them on the cross with His very own blood. He is the great and coming King who will return to Earth on a white horse to rescue us from the burdens of our own devices and to put an end to AIDS, cancer, divorce, pain, rape, murder, and death. Jesus is our Redeemer, Comforter, Husband, Bright Morning Star, and the Lamb that was slain to take away the sins of the world. He is The Way, The Truth, and The Light. He alone is our ever-present help in time of trouble. He is great and strong, beautiful and faithful. Oh, my heart is beating out of my chest to know that Jesus, only Jesus, can save us. He can save my little friend in South Africa from the pain of this world. He can save our children and their children. He can save our nation from ourselves. He is our hope, and right now in our land, we need this hope. JESUS, JESUS, JESUS. . . Nothing else will do.

Mere Men

The single greatest travesty in our land is that we have turned from trusting God. Instead of looking to Him, we have put our hope and trust in the temporary men of our time and in our own limited understanding and strength. Like the ancestors of Nehemiah, if we continue to put our trust in the mere men of our time, then our results will be the same as theirs'- more and more broken walls. Listen to the strong words of the prophet Jeremiah to the people of God during a time of great national devastation:

> *This is what the LORD says:* ***"Cursed is the one who trusts in man, who depends on flesh for his strength and whose heart turns away from the LORD.*** *He will be like a bush in the wastelands; he will not see prosperity when it comes. He will dwell in the parched places of the desert, in a salt land where no one lives.* ***"But blessed is the man who trusts in the LORD, whose confidence is in Him.*** *He will be like a tree planted by the water that sends out its roots by the stream. It does not fear when heat comes; its leaves are always green. It has no worries in a year of drought and never fails to bear fruit." Jeremiah 17:5-8*

Our trust in mere men and our dependence on "flesh for strength" has brought us a devastating spiritual curse. We have become a spiritual wasteland. Our only course of action must be to rightly place our confidence back in the God of the universe. Although God takes Israel from obscurity into greatness, they constantly turn away from Him to other nations, gods, and other kings for their safety, provision, and spirituality. God bring supernatural disaster after disaster to consume their land for the purpose of exposing the inadequacy of their own strength. Nehemiah lives in captivity because God allows His people to be overtaken in the hopes that they will return to Him for their salvation.

We are not unlike them- God alone has blessed our nation, our homes, and our churches; in return, in times of spiritual devastation, we turn to mere men for our answers. It is human nature (sin nature) for us to become satisfied with the provisions of the Lord and turn to trust the things our hands have made. But surely we can recognize by now that we are not trustworthy, and the things our hands have made do not contain the power to rescue us.

Let me give you a real life example of what I am trying to convey. Time after time in our country when we have come face to face with the issues that plague our children, we have made solid efforts in our own strength to develop programs or initiatives to bring restoration- all of them have failed. I mentioned earlier that I serve on a site-based committee at a local junior high in my hometown. A couple of years ago, we were discussing some of the "issues" the teachers and administrators were seeing in their students. We talked for an hour about the short skirts, the sagging pants, and the ways students have discovered to cheat on tests using their picture phones and text messaging. Then we began to develop a plan to battle these problems.

We discussed making the students wear uniforms and even talked about a costly device the school could purchase that would make every cell phone in the building unusable. After much time sitting quietly at the end of the table, the principal turned to me and asked me what I thought. I told him that he really did not want to know what I had to say, but he persisted. I said, "These students need Jesus. Their parents need Jesus. The problems we have discussed cannot be fixed by our programs and plotting- these are issues of the heart, and the solution can only come from the God of the heart. He is Jesus." The meeting ended quickly after that because although everyone in the room knew it was true, Jesus was not something we could ask the school planning committee to give us.

Think about it- not too long ago our "experts" came up with a solution to battle the increase in teen pregnancy in our schools. They decided to provide free condoms to students and then conducted classes on how to use them. I remember the embarrassment of several fifteen year old girls in our youth group when they were forced to practice using condoms by rolling them onto bananas in health class. I also remember thinking to myself, "This is the best we can do for a solution? Who is leading us that we think this kind of madness is the solution to our overwhelming spiritual degradation? Who was the idiot who suggested this, and why in the world did we allow it? *Is it because there is no God in [America] that we are going off to consult [experts]?* (II Kings 1:3) Must we put our trust and our children in the hands of "experts" like this?" Please tell me we are not reliant upon mere men and their programs to bring restoration to our children?

The severity of America's overwhelming infatuation with trusting everything but God was never more obvious than in our most recent presidential election. Barack Obama, who eventually won the presidency, ran on a platform of "change" and "hope." People everywhere flocked to hear him speak, and many swooned over him as if he were preparing to heal them of a sickness or save their souls. Many of the campaign rallies turned into what I would call "worship" services filled with more awe and passion than most Sunday morning church services. After the election, I saw several people wearing t-shirts that said, "Obama is my hero." All of this made me incredibly sad. This has nothing to do with Barack Obama as a person, (it could have been any man) but let me say two things: Number one- there is no man alive on this planet who can promise "change" or "hope" for our country, for our families, and for our children and make good on that promise. They do not have the power to bring true "hope" or "change." Number two- there is only one man alive worthy of being called our "hero." Unlike the mere

men of our time, He came, He died, and He overcame death
for us; His name is Jesus. We must support and pray for our
leaders as prescribed by the Bible, but we cannot look to
them as our source of hope, change, or salvation.

Listen to me. Dr. Phil cannot save us. Oprah cannot save
us. The President of the United Sates cannot save us. Our
military, though the greatest in the world, is made up of mere
men, and they cannot save us. The Psalmists tells us that,
*"No king is saved by the size of his army; no warrior escapes
by his great strength"* (Psalm 33:16). The greatest men and
women of our time are no match for the devastation sin has
brought into our land. They are not equipped to reconstruct
the spiritual walls of our nation. Your children, my children,
and the spiritual Orphas of our America are no different than
my little friend in South Africa- only Jesus can cure their
disease. We must remember God; nothing else will do.

Nehemiah starts his prayer by remembering that God
is the only source for healing, wholeness, and restoration.
Our lives as followers of the Lord should be bowed before
God to say, "You are God, we are Your children, and we are
in desperate need of You- no one else will do." The broken
world does not need another sermon or self-help book from
some "expert." We need an encounter with the living God of
the universe. If you stop reading right now, and from this day
forward you make it your heart's cry to remember God- your
life and the lives of those God has called you to spiritually
parent we forever be different.

Mom, your son needs Jesus; his education will not save
him. Dad, your daughter needs Jesus, not a man with a good
career. Teacher, your students need Jesus, not better text-
books. Coach, your team needs Jesus, not a winning record.
Pastor, your flock needs Jesus, not your educated opinion.
Church, the lost need Jesus, not our cutting edge, cultur-
ally-relevant, seeker-sensitive services. Rebuilders, the next
generation needs Jesus, so you and I must call on Him. We

must cry out to Jesus, Jesus, Jesus. He is faithful; He is able, and He is willing to restore those who will come to Him in humility and brokenness.

This is our "Declaration of Dependence." We are at our wit's end, we call on You, oh great and awesome God, to come and rescue us- no one else will do."

Do not put your trust in princes, in mortal men, who cannot save. When their spirit departs, they return to the ground; on that very day their plans come to nothing. Blessed is he whose help is the God of Jacob, whose hope is in the LORD his God, the Maker of Heaven and Earth, the sea, and everything in them- the LORD, who remains faithful forever. He upholds the cause of the oppressed and gives food to the hungry. The LORD sets prisoners free, the LORD gives sight to the blind, the LORD lifts up those who are bowed down, the LORD loves the righteous. The LORD watches over the alien and sustains the fatherless and the widow, but He frustrates the ways of the wicked. The LORD reigns forever, your God, O Zion, for all generations. Praise the LORD. Psalms 146:3-10

Chapter Fourteen

Land of the Proud

At the root of almost every sin is a single, common denominator- Pride. America is considered the "Land of the Proud." This is a devastating problem for our country because God has a very distinct reaction to pride- He hates it. If we are going to declare a "Declaration of Dependence" then the "Land of the Proud" must understand God's feelings about pride. There are a few hundred Bible verses where God reveals His heart concerning the issue of pride. These are just a few of them but enough for us to get the picture.

I, wisdom, dwell together with prudence; I possess knowledge and discretion. To fear the LORD is to hate evil; ***I hate pride and arrogance****, evil behavior and perverse speech. Proverbs 8:12-13*

Love the LORD, all his saints! The LORD preserves the faithful, but the ***proud*** *He pays back in full. Psalms 31:23*

The LORD detests all the ***proud*** *of heart. Be sure of this: They will not go unpunished. Proverbs 16:5*

The LORD Almighty has a day in store for all the **proud** *and lofty, for all that is exalted (and they will be humbled). Isaiah 2:12*

Live in harmony with one another. Do not be **proud**, *but be willing to associate with people of low position. Do not be conceited. Romans 12:16*

*"**God opposes the proud** but gives grace to the humble." I Peter 5:5*

The Bible is very clear about how God views and handles anyone who approaches Him in pride- He hates the proud and stands in opposition to them. When we are walking in pride, we are truly standing as an opponent of the Lord. We are in battle with Him; a battle we cannot win. Pride is what gets satan kicked out of Heaven and is the motive behind Adam and Eve's first encounter with sin. Pride is our enemy; it is at the root of our spiritual brokenness.

It is often pride that keeps us glued to our chair on Sunday mornings when God is calling us to go forward in repentance. It is pride keeping us from the marriage counseling that can rebuild the walls of our families. Pride causes our lives to be filled with bitterness over wrongs we do not bring ourselves to forgive, even though we have been forgiven of our own ugly shortcomings. It is pride that causes us to refuse the helping hand of God in our broken state. Pride is often at the root of our anger towards those called to rebuke us. It causes us to build bigger barns, bigger houses, and bigger bank accounts while the world starves to death around us. Pride causes us to tout the greatness of our own success rather than giving God the glory due Him. Pride has destroyed kings and castles, marriages and families, churches and governments, and if we are not able to rightly dispose of it, then it WILL destroy us as well. Pride tricks us into believing we can be our own gods. We are horrible gods, and we have proven it over and over again. Every time I turn on the evening news, I am reminded that we are not qualified to be our own gods.

Pride turns the ear of God away from our cries, and provokes Him to anger. Here is why: He will not accept anything less than being God. He is in control. He is sovereign; He is above us and greater than we are. He is the Potter, and we are the clay. Pride causes us to lose the proper perspective of who we are compared to who God is. He is above us; we are under Him. When we refuse to acknowledge Him as supreme in our lives, we stand in opposition to Him. When we presume to know better for our lives than He does, we have become just as Adam and Eve, even as satan. We may be able to send a man to the moon, but we will never be the God who created the entire universe with mere words. If we are so arrogant to think we do not need the God of the universe, then we are in serious trouble. I cannot overstate the devastation pride has brought to our land. It makes my heart sick and brings me great trepidation to watch the leaders of our country stand before our nation in arrogance and proclaim *our* greatness, without even a mention of the God who truly sustains us.

When I was ordained into the ministry, my grandfather passed on to me the Bible given him during his ordination in 1947. Inside the front flap was written this quote, "I tremble for my countrymen when I remember that God is just." The quote was said by Thomas Jefferson and then repeated by Abraham Lincoln. We cannot poke our chest out at the God of the universe and then expect Him to smile upon our arrogance. The Bible is full of nations, including the nation of Israel, who refused to humble themselves before God- He crushed them all. Our country is known around the world for being a people of incredible arrogance. Sadly, we also carry the claim of being a "Christian" nation. These two things can never go hand in hand. They are opposites. Pride is opposite of Christ-likeness. Pride is opposite of love. Pride is opposite of God. Do not be deceived; pride is not the banner we should fly over our children or our nation. The pride of the American people, including the American "Christian," is at the very core of the destruction of our spiritual walls. God cannot be for us if we continue to walk in pride.

Jesus was sent to the Earth to be the ultimate example of humility. He came off His throne in the glory of Heaven to be beaten and brutally murdered by His very own creation. The first time He came was to provide redemption, a way to the Father through death and resurrection, but when He returns, He will be riding a white horse, carrying the sword of God, and wearing a white robe dipped in blood to pass judgment on the proud, vile, detestable, and all who have refused His sacrifice (Revelation 19:11-16). Then we will see Him as He truly is- King above all Kings, Lord above all Lords, Creator, Sustainer, Holy and Anointed, Majestic, Unstoppable, Immeasurable, The Devouring Lion of the Tribe of Judah.

Let me give you just a few examples of the results of prideful leadership in the Bible. II Chronicles twenty-six details the story of one of the great kings of the nation of Judah. Uzziah was an incredible leader and became one of the most powerful men in the world because he walked in the favor of the God of Heaven, *"but after Uzziah became powerful, his pride led to his downfall" (II Chronicles 26:16).* He died a leper. Following in his footsteps was another king named Hezekiah. He also became great by the Lord's favor, *"But Hezekiah's heart was proud and he did not respond to the kindness shown him; therefore the LORD'S wrath was on him and on Judah and Jerusalem" (II Chronicles 32:25).*

We cannot forget Nebuchadnezzar whom God allowed to lead the Babylonians in crushing Jerusalem and enslaving the Jews. In his pride we see that, *"As the king was walking on the roof of the royal palace of Babylon, he said, 'Is not* *this the great Babylon **I have built** as the royal residence, by **my mighty power** and for the glory of **my majesty**?' 'This is what is decreed for you, King Nebuchadnezzar: Your royal authority has been taken from you. You will be driven away from people and will live with the wild animals; you will eat grass like cattle. Seven times will pass by for you until you acknowledge that the Most High is sovereign over the kingdoms of men and gives them to anyone he wishes'" (Daniel 4:29-32).* Nebuchadnezzar spent the next seven years living in the fields eating grass like cattle until he relented that his accomplishments were only possible by the hand of the God of Heaven. You get the picture. The results of prideful leadership are devastating; the broken walls in the Bible and of America are proof.

We Can't

When my son Kaiden was about three years old, God rearranged my understanding of this very subject. A preacher friend of mine was at the house, and we were just visiting about life, ministry, and missions. My son and I were tossing the football back and forth; it was one of those hard plastic balls the cheerleaders throw out into the crowd at football games on Friday nights here in Texas. Kaiden was really struggling to catch the ball. Truthfully, it was hitting him in the face every time I threw it to him. Before too long, I became frustrated with him. I mean we are an athletic family, and Kaiden was putting on a pathetic showing for my friend. (Did I mention he was three?) Finally, I snapped and gruffly told him if he did not catch the ball, then he would be in trouble with me. The next thing that came out of Kaiden's mouth was life-changing. He said, "Daddy, I can't catch it." I was beside myself. Like all good ole' West Texas grown boys, I told him what I heard a million times growing up: "Boy, we do not say those words in this house. We never say 'I can't.' You know better than that. Get down and give me ten push-ups right now." With tears in his eyes, Kaiden immediately hit the ground and began to do the best push-ups a three year old could do.

As I was trying not to explode, my "friend" chimed in, "That is real good theology preacher." My head almost popped off. I could not believe he was telling me how to rear *my* son in *my* house. (Can you see the incredible pride spewing out of me?) What my friend said next changed my life, my son's life, my ministry, my marriage, and my heart forever. He said, "Well Kevin, I will just put it to you this way- If your son cannot learn to say, 'I can't,' then he will never have a relationship with Jesus." Wow! It took me a second to process what he was saying. The truth of his rebuke broke me in half. The pride in my heart melted away as I watched my son struggle to live out his father's arrogance.

Salvation, restoration, and rebuilding are all about the understanding that "we can't." We could never have paid for our own sin, conquered death, nor done enough good to ensure us the perfection that an entrance to Heaven requires. I picked my young son up from the ground, hugged him, wiped the tears from his eyes, and told him that I was an idiot. I shared with him the truth about me- that I am small and weak and cannot do anything of significance in my own power. I shared with him how the God of Heaven and Earth is big, strong, and willing to do the significant things for me. I told him that because I could not save myself, He sent His son Jesus to rescue me- to rescue him. I can't- We can't- He already has.

Now listen, I am not training my son to be a quitter in any way because the Bible teaches us that whatever we do in word or deed, we should do it as if we are doing it unto the Lord (Colossians 3:17). We should do everything with excellence and not shrink back. We are called to be people who stand strong in the face of adversity. The difference is found in the source of our strength. We do not stand in our own power, but in the shelter and sovereignty of the God who created all things. **Just as we must recognize the truth of the brokenness of our current reality, we must also recognize that in our own strength, we cannot change it.** The key to a strong marriage is our willingness to ask God to make it great. The key to properly training our children is contingent upon us coming to God honestly and declaring that we cannot offer them anything good except for Him. The key to reestablishing the spiritual walls in our families, churches, and our country can be found in this single principal.

Since that time, my son and I have worked out a deal about this subject in our own lives. Because we recognize the severe hatred of God towards the proud, we hold each other accountable. If Kaiden sees me becoming puffed up with pride, he simply says to me, "Hey dad, you know what comes before the fall right?" It is embarrassing when your son has to be the person who reminds you that pride always comes before the fall, but it is much better than the fall. The land of the proud will never be the land of the free. God opposes the proud and promises that until we learn to humble ourselves at His feet, the walls will just keep falling down.

Exalts the Humble

It is our humility before a holy God that brings about great revival and restoration. As God opposes the proud, He rescues and exalts the humble. God is The Father who stands ready to rescue His children when they cry out to Him in desperation and humility. He stands ready to rebuild for those who understand their proper position in His hands-we are the clay. Let's take it even a step further. God seeks humility, and He is **actively seeking** to restore those who come to Him with a contrite heart.

This is what the LORD says: "Heaven is My throne, and the Earth is My footstool. Where is the house you will build for Me? Where will My resting place be? Has not My hand made all these things, and so they came into being?" declares the LORD. "This is the one I esteem: he who is humble and contrite in spirit, and trembles at My word."
Isaiah 66:1-2

Time and again in scripture, it is the humility of God's people, even of God's enemies, that turns the heart of God from opposing them to rescuing them. Do you remember the people of Nineveh that Jonah begrudgingly warned about God's coming destruction? At the time of Jonah's rebuke, the city of Nineveh was the greatest city in the known world. It is said that the walls of the city were one hundred feet high and sixty miles around, taking 1.5 million men eight years to build. In the midst of all their greatness, upon hearing the warning, the great king of Nineveh took off his royal robes and clothed himself in sackcloth. He bowed down in the dirt before a God he had not served. He declared that the entire city follow his leadership by fasting, calling urgently on God, and turning from their evil ways in hopes God might have mercy on them. God did.

I want you to see it this way. The king of the greatest city in the world took off his royal robes (his pride), and clothed himself in sackcloth (humility). In essence, he took off his armor, laid down his sword, and came humbly before God. While wearing his armor and his royal robes, he was in opposition to the Lord. But when he became vulnerable, humiliated himself, and surrendered to God, the Creator of the universe had mercy on him and restored his city. This is the exact kind of leadership we need in our families, churches, and cities today. We must bow down in humility before a Holy God that He might grant us mercy and restore our walls. We must surrender ourselves to His leadership.

Pride equals broken walls; humility equals restored walls. It truly is that simple. King David is one of the greatest examples of a man constantly restored in the Bible. After he is found guilty of adultery and murder, he humbles himself before God and honors God with these words: *You do not delight in sacrifice, or I would bring it; you do not take pleasure in burnt offerings. The sacrifices of God are a broken spirit;* ***a broken and contrite heart, O God, you will not despise*** *(Psalms 51:16-17)*.

David, like Nehemiah, Daniel, Paul, and many others in the scripture understands that God exalts the humble. He rebuilds, restores, and is constantly looking to revive the humble. David knows that, *"The LORD sustains the humble but casts the wicked to the ground" (Psalms 147:6)*. This understanding is what makes David a man after God's own heart. Our healing, our restoration, our rebuilding effort for the coming generations is contingent upon our understanding that God alone is big. He alone is worthy, and He alone is our faithful Savior and Redeemer. Fathers, mothers, pastors, and leaders of every kind must be willing to humble themselves before the Lord if we truly desire revival and restoration.

We must stop teaching the coming generations to "pull themselves up by their bootstraps" and begin teaching them to humble themselves before the Lord. We must stop teaching them about the self-centered, pride-driven idea called the "American Dream" and begin teaching them the "Declaration of Dependence." Rather than put together another theory on how to solve the latest crisis, we must fall facedown before God and declare ourselves weak and small. It is time for us to recognize we are the clay, and call out to our potter for restoration. The greatest among us are those willing to be the least. They will be exalted by the Lord. I am learning to be the least, but I find myself prone to much arrogance and wrong thinking. Paul reminds the Corinthians, and me, that *"The man who thinks he knows something does not yet know as he ought to know. But the man who loves God is known by God" (I Corinthians 8:2-3).* I want to be known by God. Which man are you? The man who thinks he knows something or the man who loves God- you cannot be both.

Deceleration of Dependence

Allow me to give you one last example of the kind of humble and godly leadership we must seek for our families, churches, and our nation if we truly desire to see the walls repaired. In II Chronicles twenty, Jehoshaphat, the great king of Judah, finds himself and his entire nation facing the Moabites and Ammonites. He recognizes that his army is no match for the enemy he is facing. He declares a fast for all of Judah to inquire of the Lord; men, women, and children stand together to seek the face of their God. Jehoshaphat makes this declaration of dependence, *"For we have no power to face this vast army that is attacking us. **We do not know what to do, but our eyes are upon you.**"* Through the prophet Jahaziel, the Lord responds by saying, *"Do not be afraid or discouraged because of this vast army, for the battle is not yours, but God's."* The Lord destroys the army of the Moabites and the Ammonites before the army of Judah even reaches them.

We face a seemingly overwhelming and powerful enemy. He has convinced many of us that we are too far gone, too broken, and that all hope is lost. All of those things are true if we rely upon ourselves, but we must make a Declaration of Dependence- the declaration of Jehoshaphat and the people of God: "We do know what to do, but our eyes are upon You, King Jesus." It gives me chills just thinking about it. We serve the great and awesome God, the battle belongs to Him, but He will not move on our behalf until we come to Him in humility and brokenness.

Chapter Fifteen

Repent

Nehemiah humbles himself before the Lord, fasts, and desperately cries out to the Lord acknowledging that only He can heal the brokenness of his people. Next, he does something to awaken the restorative heart of God - he repents. He agrees with God that he and the nation of Israel have sinned against God. He understands that his sin and the sins of his people are the reasons for the devastation in Jerusalem and commits to putting a stop to it. He decides to call the people of God back to the laws and decrees of their heavenly Father. Look at his words unto the Lord:

> *Let your ear be attentive and your eyes open to hear the prayer your servant is praying before You day and night for your servants, the people of Israel. **I confess the sins we Israelites, including myself and my father's house, have committed against you.** We have acted very wickedly toward You. We have not obeyed the commands, decrees and laws You gave your servant Moses. Nehemiah 1:6-7*

I want to take this opportunity to partner the prayer of Nehemiah with the very words of the prophet Daniel, so we can get an understanding of the significance of their humility and repentance before the Lord. After learning the captivity of the Jews in Babylon will last some seventy years, the Bible tells us that Daniel "*turns to the Lord God and pleads with Him in prayer and petition, in fasting and in sackcloth and ashes*" (Daniel 9). Look at the similarities of his prayer to the prayer of Nehemiah.

> *O Lord, the great and awesome God, who keeps His covenant of love with all who love Him and obey His commands, **we have sinned and done wrong**. We have been wicked and have rebelled; we have turned away from Your commands and laws. We have not listened to Your servants the prophets, who spoke in Your name to our kings, our princes and our fathers, and to all the people of the land. Daniel 9:4-6*

Daniel, like Nehemiah, understands that true repentance awakens the heart of God to the cry of His people. They both understand sin is at the root of the devastation and are willing to do whatever it takes to bring their people back into a right relationship with God. Repentance is not too popular a preaching topic these days, but of all the lessons Jesus came to Earth to teach, He starts with a very simple sermon about repentance. Here is how it goes:

"Repent for the kingdom of Heaven is at hand."

There it is, the next step in the process. We must *recognize* our need for a Savior; we must assume *responsibility* for our actions; we must *respond* in brokenness; we must *remember* the faithfulness of God, and then we must *repent* of our wrong thinking, wrong living, and wrong hearts. **Without repentance, there is no restoration.** Let us look at the word "repent" in a couple of different contexts. The word "repent" Jesus uses here in Matthew 4:17 has several different meanings. The most obvious is simply to stop going one direction, turn around, and start going the other. In one of its most literal translations as Jesus used it, the word "repent" also means to "re-think" or "think differently." Both of these understandings are appropriate for us today and need to be applied to our lives and rebuilding efforts, so let's talk through them both.

Turn

Let me ask you a question? If you knew for sure the direction you are headed today would eventually lead you to destruction, would you keep going that way? Of course not, but still we find ourselves doing exactly that. It is obvious the direction we have been going as a nation has not led us to revival, but still we continue on the same path to destruction. Both Nehemiah and Daniel understand this. They too have seen their people choose the wrong road, but they also know the only way to find restoration is by admitting they have not followed the decrees of the Lord- by admitting their sin.

We have no record of Nehemiah nor Daniel committing grave sins against the Lord, yet both of them come to God in humility and repent; this is the kind of leadership needed for restoration. Instead of blaming the "world" for the devastation we find ourselves living in, we must look within ourselves. We must ask God to show us the directions we have been going that are opposite of His leading. We must also agree with God that He alone is good and that our righteousness outside of Him is as filthy rags (Isaiah 64:6). We must then come honestly before Him about the personal sin in our own lives and repent for our own complacency, arrogance, selfishness, and distrust of Him. Finally, we must personally ask God to give us each a new direction for every part of our lives.

Both Nehemiah and Daniel do something else that is very interesting; they not only repent for themselves, but they admit their nation has not obeyed the commands of the Lord. They recognize that national repentance is the key to national restoration. Revival, the rebuilding effort, starts in one heart, in my heart and in your heart, but our repentance must work its way into our families, our churches, and our cities. Once again, these men show incredible, godly leadership. They want to see God do something miraculous; they recognize that He is the only God who can. In intercession, they readily admit their own sin and the sin of their nation, calling on Him to act. As the physical walls are rebuilt in Jerusalem, the people of God follow Nehemiah's example of repentance with an incredible movement of national confession that puts into motion an incredible spiritual revival. The Bible says that *"They stood in their places and confessed their sins and the wickedness of their fathers. They stood where they were and read from the Book of the Law of the LORD their God for a quarter of the day, and spent another quarter in confession and in worshiping the LORD their God." (Nehemiah 9:2-3).*

Like the Jews of Nehemiah's time, America has not followed the commands of the God of the Bible. We cannot continue to walk in sin as a people and then in arrogance raise our flag and ask God to bless our land. Repentance is our declaration to God that His way is right and our way is futile. My family, my church, my city- we have disobeyed God in many ways. We are wicked and depraved, and outside of the Lord, we have no good thing to offer. **Recognition of sin produces brokenness; brokenness produces repentance; repentance produces restoration.** *"Godly sorrow brings repentance that leads to salvation and leaves no regret" (2Corinthians 7:10).*

We owe the God who rescued us from the hand of tyranny an apology. We owe the children following us an apology.

Just as we were taught to do at an early age, we need to say, "I'm sorry. We are sorry for the mess we have made." We must prove our repentance by committing ourselves to turning from our sinful ways and rebuilding the torn down areas of our nation. Our Godly sorrow will bring repentance that leads to salvation, restoration, and revival. The repentant man is always being restored, and he walks closely with the God who brings life and revival; the same can be said for the repentant nation. Fathers, mothers, coaches, and pastors: here is where we gain the power, provision, and the passion to rebuild. In humility before the Father, we admit we have sinned and fallen short. In turn, the Lord restores us through the full work of the cross where Jesus took upon Himself the sin of the world. Only then will He begin to use us to rebuild what the enemy has destroyed.

> *If we claim to be without sin, we deceive ourselves and the truth is not in us. If we confess our sins, He is faithful and just and will forgive us our sins and purify us from all unrighteousness. If we claim we have not sinned, we make Him out to be a liar and His word has no place in our lives. I John 1:8-10*

I love it; so much is said in this passage. He is faithful and just to forgive our sins. Just in case we feel we are not in need of repentance, John reminds us, "*If we claim we have not sinned, we make Him out to be a liar and His word has no place in our lives.*" We have all sinned and are all in desperate need of repentance. Surely we can agree by now that the direction we are leading the coming generations is not the direction God would have us take them. At some point, if we desire revival, we must stop dishonoring God and turn from our wickedness. Something has to change; it is that simple.

Let me give you an example of how repentance can bring about great change on our planet. Everyday around the world, almost 16,000 children die from hunger-related causes; that means one child dies every five seconds.[14] Most of us are aware of this epidemic by now, but think about it this way-world hunger is a choice, not of those who are starving, but of those who have plenty. It cost an estimated $75 to feed a child for an entire year in most third world countries. In America, we pay guys upwards of $25,000,000 per year to throw a baseball, catch a football, or act in a movie- to entertain us. Do the math. In the two-hour span it takes to watch a motion picture, 1,440 children will die of hunger.

Let me take it a step further. In the year 2000, the total annual cost of the obesity problem in America was $117,000,000,000.[15] While millions of children die each year around the world from not having enough to eat, we are spending hundreds of billions of dollars to fix health problems in this country related to eating too much. I cannot even process the unpalatable truth of this reality. We allow world hunger to exist. We have the resources in our country to put a stop to the millions of hunger-related deaths a year, but we choose not to. Jesus declares that what we do to the least of these: the hungry, the naked, and the imprisoned, we do unto Him (Matthew 25). God judges the validity of our faith based on these things. Ignoring a world in need is sin- sin we must repent of and change. At some point, if we truly desire to see change, we must change. It is not enough to simply talk about how "sad" these situations are. We have a scriptural mandate to not only recognize sin, but to make a personal change. Our spiritual walls are broken, and if we want to see them repaired, we must turn from the things destroying them. Turn!

I need to point out something very significant about sin. As a preacher, I get asked some really crazy questions, most of which I cannot answer. These are some common ones: "Why do babies die? Why does God allow hurricanes, cancer, or events like 9/11?" For the longest time, I struggled to answer these kinds of questions until the day Orpha died and I found myself asking God the exact same things. He answered me very clearly: Sin. Sin destroys our world. I am not saying my sin causes something bad to happen to someone I love or the sin of a certain city causes a hurricane. What I am saying is that sin, a complete disregard for the commandments of the Lord, is the exact reason our world is broken. Sin destroys all things. Death is a product of sin.

Go back to the very beginning. In Genesis chapter three, in a moment of complete pride and disregard for the commands of the Lord, the human race invites all the brokenness possible into the world; brokenness we are still experiencing today. Until we decided to be our own gods, there was no cancer, no pain, no murder, no hurricanes, and no death. We are living in a world we built for ourselves, but God, who is rich in mercy, sent His Son to die in our place. He redeems us, so one day we can start over without the ability to invite the brokenness of sin into our world. In that time, there will be no pain or mourning, tears or death for those who have received the Son and rightly repented of their sin (Revelation 21:1-5).

Sin is not cute or harmless in any way. Sin is serious, and its results are horrifying, but God is faithful and just to forgive those who repent in humility and brokenness. If you have ever watched someone fight and lose a battle with cancer, looked into the eyes of a young mother whose husband went to war and did not come back, felt the grip of father's arms whose son has just taken his own life, reached out your hand to a young girl who has had her innocence snatched from her by the perversion of a man, or kissed the face of baby orphaned by AIDS, then you have come face to face with the devastation of sin. We must learn to hate the results of sin enough to stop it, enough to repent. *Hate what is evil, cling to what is good. Romans 12:9*

Rethink

Let's look at the "re-think" side of repentance. "Rethink for the Kingdom of God is at hand." Jesus is simply telling the Jews they must begin to think differently than they have been thinking. They *think* the King of Jews will establish an earthly kingdom; Jesus tells them to *rethink* that idea because He came to establish an eternal kingdom (John 18:36). They *think* that as long as things look good on the outside, they are fine. Jesus tells them to *rethink* that too because God sees the heart of a man and judges his motives (Matthew 23:25-28). Repeatedly in the gospels, Jesus implores the Jews to stop thinking one direction and start thinking another- to start thinking as He does.

Let's just walk through a couple of areas where we are in need of repentance, or re-thinking, as a nation:

We think children are a burden (hence the 45 million abortions), but the Bible teaches us that children are a gift from the Lord (Psalm 127). Many of us need to repent for seeing our children, or any children for that matter, as a burden instead of a gift. When we start agreeing with God that children are a blessing rather than a burden, our hearts will be committed to seeing them rescued. We will be inspired by the heart of God to protect the vulnerable and defend the weak. When we think as He does, everything changes. *Oh God please forgive us for brutally murdering our own children through abortion, for abandoning them on the altar of worldly success, and for not protecting against the flaming darts of the enemy. Oh God, please have mercy on us and please help us change the culture of our country. RETHINK!*

We think we can rebuild on our own, but the Bible tells us that apart from the Lord, we can do nothing (John 15:5). We must cry out to God for His help and repent for thinking we can gain spiritual success on our own. We can't, but we serve the God who can. *RETHINK!*

We think tomorrow is a guarantee, so we move about with no sense of urgency, but the Bible tells us we must always be prepared because the end will come like a thief in the night (I Thessalonians 5:2). We need to repent for allowing ourselves to become apathetic in our pursuit of the Lord and our training of the next generation. We must live and worship, teach and love as if everyday were the last day, for our lives are as a vapor- here today and then gone away. (James 4:14) *RETHINK!*

We think church membership is more important than discipleship, but the Bible clearly says our purpose on this planet is to bring God glory by making disciples of all nations. I cannot remember the Bible saying anything at all about "church" membership. Many of us need to repent for desiring to build our own kingdoms rather than the kingdom of God. We must learn to think as Jesus does. The church is about growing the people not the property. There may be some who would argue that this is not a valid issue for the Church of God; however, the millions of dollars worth of empty church buildings in our country are a direct result of this kind of thinking. Yes, we may need buildings to meet in, and we should never forsake the gathering of the brethren, but when we spend more time, money, and energy on the building campaign than we do on discipleship, we have proven our need for repentance. *RETHINK!*

We, as leaders, think we can say one thing and do another, but Romans 2:17-24 tells us when we say one thing and do another we give the world cause to blaspheme our God. This is one of the major reasons the American "church" has no credibility. We must repent for our hypocrisy and seek to live lives that mirror the teaching of the Lord. We must change our habits, our priorities, and the example we are setting for those following us. Then when the Church gets ready to say something, the world will listen. *RETHINK!*

The need for "rethinking" is as true for us today as in the days of Jesus' ministry on the Earth. He places value on the eternal; we place value on the temporary. He calls us into passionate relationship; we teach religious obligation. He calls the children unto Him and tells us to be like them in faith; we put the children outside the sanctuary so they will not be a distraction to the "service." Repentance is about learning to think according to the teachings of the Word of God. We have to learn to hate the things He hates, to love the things He loves, and to arrange our priorities according to His character, not our own.

We start by *rethinking* the way we do life especially in the context of the discipling the next generation. **If we believe the Bible then those beliefs should change how we think, and how we think should change how we live.** I would love for us to take some time right this minute to ask God to expose the areas in our lives we should be repentant of today. Nehemiah and Daniel both give us great examples why we should come before the Lord in prayer and fasting and they demonstrate how to do it for us. This is our chance to come humbly before the great and awesome God together and declare our dependence, admit our sin, and ask God for the restoration of our spiritual walls.

Take this time to come honestly before your Father in Heaven. He is a great and merciful God, and He loves you. He wants to rebuild the spiritual walls falling down in your life. He wants to restore your family, your marriage, your children, your church, and your city. Make today the first day of many where you come humbly, honestly, in brokenness, and with a repentant heart before the Father. He is faithful and just to forgive us and purify us. Let us just cry out to Him together.

(You can use the space at the end of this chapter or at the end of the book to write out your own prayer of repentance before our Holy and merciful God today.)

Section Six

Risk

Chapter Sixteen

You are Nehemiah

I wish I could reach through this book and hug your neck. I hope none of you want to reach through it and wring mine, but I am glad we are in this together. I want to share the next piece of Nehemiah's blueprint. After Nehemiah prays for four months, after he fasts, humbles himself, and repents for his own sin and the sin of his people, he does something remarkable. By the Lord's leading, Nehemiah decides he is the one God has chosen to rebuild the walls of the city of Jerusalem. Indeed, he is the one who needs to go there and restore the name of the Lord.

Here is the problem: He happens to work for a king who has already crushed the rebuilding effort in Jerusalem some thirteen years earlier, and if he goes to the king with a request of any kind, the king could put him to death without a question. Nehemiah is taking a huge risk. He is literally putting his life on the line for the name of God and the people of the next generation.

You are Nehemiah.

For too long when confronted with the overwhelming devastation of the future generations in our country, many of us look to our neighbor, church organizations, the school system, or the government for our revival. We need look no further than ourselves. The discipleship of the future rests on the people of God. Rebuilding is going to cost us, but we must be willing to risk it all to make King Jesus known and see our children walk with the Lord. Most every parent would risk their life to save the life of their child physically; unfortunately, saving them physically will not save them spiritually. They will face eternity. There is nothing worthier of our lives than seeing the next generation walk with Jesus. It will require incredible amounts of time, energy, resources, and faith, but we must make it the priority of our lives to see the walls rebuilt. Like Joshua, Abraham, Paul, Peter, and the martyr Steven, we must be willing to follow the Lord wherever He may lead us.

Jesus clearly explains what is required of us if we want to be called His followers and teach the next generation how to follow Him- we must die daily and take up our cross and follow Him (Matthew 16:24). **We must be more afraid of the results of not following God than the results of following Him.** *Don't be afraid of them. Remember the Lord, who is great and awesome, and fight for your brothers, your sons and your daughters, your wives and your homes (Nehemiah 4:14).* You may need to quit your job, move to another city, begin marriage counseling, or simply rearrange your priorities. Whatever the case, we must be willing to do whatever it takes to redeem the Bride of Christ.

Nehemiah is willing. He goes before the king knowing he could lose his life, but he trusts God for it all, and God is on his side. The pagan king not only allows him to go back to rebuild Jerusalem, he also sends with him a letter securing his safety from other enemies. He provides him with the lumber to rebuild the walls, an army to protect him, and the resources to complete the process. God is on the side of those who seek to glorify Him and carry out His commission. Jesus said that as we go to make disciples, he would be with us until the end of the age (Matthew 28:20). God is about restoration, and He stands with those who are about Him. As we move into the section of the book providing the actual rebuilding tools, we must each declare before God that no matter the cost, we will bring Him glory by fulfilling His commission for those who follow us.

Section Seven

Let Us Rebuild

Chapter Seventeen

The Home Front

Then I said to them, "You see the trouble we are in: Jerusalem lies in ruins, and its gates have been burned with fire. **Come, let us rebuild the wall of Jerusalem, and we will no longer be in disgrace."** *I also told them about the gracious hand of my God upon me and what the king had said to me. They replied,* **"Let us start rebuilding."** *So they began this good work. Nehemiah 2:17-18*

Here we go. *"Let us start rebuilding."* Nehemiah arrives in Jerusalem and after assessing the condition of the walls and the people, he gathers the willing Jews to start the process of rebuilding. Nehemiah and the people begin the process of rebuilding the city walls in chapter three, giving us great insight as to exactly how and where we should start.

Eliashib the high priest and his fellow priests went to work and rebuilt the Sheep Gate. They dedicated it and set its doors in place, building as far as the Tower of the Hundred, which they dedicated, and as far as the Tower of Hananel. The men of Jericho built

the adjoining section, and Zaccur son of Imri built
next to them. Nehemiah 3:1-2

Notice the first people mentioned in the rebuilding effort
are the high priest and his fellow priest. There are a couple
of really important things here for us to learn. Number one:
The Church is at the center, the forefront of the process of
rebuilding. For us, this is of the utmost importance; we must
know and understand that the Church is indeed the hope of
the world. We are the family of God called to disciple the next
generation. We are the one, true family with the resources,
power, authority, and love needed to rebuild the families
and cities of America. One of the great prophetic preachers
of our time, Adrian Rogers once said, "The revival of our
country will not come through the White House, the court
house, or the school house, it will come through the **church
house.**" He was preaching a sermon on II Chronicles 7:14
about America's need to humble ourselves before God and
cry out for the coming generations. This verse is the foundation of everything we are seeking:

If my people, who are called by my name, will
humble themselves and pray and seek my face and
turn from their wicked ways, then will I hear from
Heaven and will forgive their sin and will heal their
land. II Chronicles 7:14

If my people...The Church, the family of God, must lead
the way in the rebuilding effort. Our leadership must personally commit to the commission of God. Pastors and church
leaders everywhere must begin to treat the current devastation of our spiritual walls as the emergency it truly is. We
are in a position to bring it to the forefront of the minds and
hearts of the families we serve. Simply put- we need our
church leaders to make the rescuing and training of the next

generation priority in our local churches. How can we make disciples of all nations if we are not even making disciples in our nation? If you are a church leader in any capacity, it is past time for us to become the voice of rebuilding for the next generation. We need to dedicate our prayers, time, resources, and our very lives to this process and lead our people rightly according to the commission given us by God. If the Church does not take a leading role in the restoration of the next generation, there will be no restoration.

Home Team

Last summer, I spent a month on the road preaching at youth camps. During that month, I heard three separate stories of men in the ministry recently caught in the act of adultery. These are not the stories making big headlines like many of the situations involving prominent preachers, but they are an indicator of a trend contributing to the crumbling of our spiritual walls. Our pastors and church leaders are dying on the vine, and their families are dying along with them. This breaks my heart. The enemy has waged a huge attack on the men who lead our churches, and we must begin to take back some ground on a personal level with our own families and our own walks with the Lord. The emerging of the corporate church has brought with it the woes of the corporate world for our leaders. Pastors, youth pastors, church leaders- you and I must first be able to rightly love our wives and disciple our own children. There is nothing more important, and I truly mean nothing, than the very welfare of our own marriages and children. This is how we lead the people of the church into rebuilding their own homes, by being proactive in rebuilding ours.

We should all be aware of the Biblical mandate for leadership in the Church. For those of us who are pastors or leaders of any kind, we must understand that God is judging us based not on how many people are in the pews on Sunday morning, but on how our very own children view us. The litmus test for us is not the fervor with which we fill the pulpit, but the fervor with which we rightly love and disciple our own families. You may need to call the church office right now and tell them you are going to need some time off because as their leader, you need to work on some things spiritually on the "home team." This is the kind of leadership our churches and families are in need of today. Let us lead the process of reconstruction by example in our own homes and make it clear to those who follow us that we are committed to living out the word of God outside of the pulpit. Our marriages must be strong (not perfect), our personal relationship with Jesus must be intimate, and our children must be priority. Until we have taken the time, energy, and effort to secure things with the "home team," we will be ineffective in leading God's people in revival. Until we have done those things, we have no business leading at all.

News Flash- Sheep Killing Shepherds at Alarming Rates

Before I walked into my first interview for a youth ministry position with the church personnel committee, a pastor friend of mine gave me some much-needed advice. He told me I would need two things: a shovel and a life jacket. I had no idea what he was talking about until I discovered that all the church expects of its leaders is for them to raise people from the dead and walk on water. People of the Church- Your leaders are only as good as their homes and marriages, so please give them a chance to actually spend some time and energy working to improve their families. I have personally watched twelve men, including several seminary graduates, get completely, spiritually destroyed working inside the church.

We must remember our leaders are just like us- sinners saved by grace with spouses and children who are in desperate need of their fathers and mothers. Unfortunately, some of the most spiritually-orphaned children in the world live in the parsonages of our churches. This is completely unacceptable. Our leaders need to spend time and energy training their own families, but we must give them the opportunity to. We need to learn to admonish and support our leaders in such a way that they feel not only free to love their spouses and children rightly, but are also inspired to do so.

Obey your leaders and submit to them, for they keep watch over your souls as those who will give an account. **Let them do this with joy and not with grief, for this would be unprofitable for you.** *Hebrews 13:17*

This is truly a cry from my heart to the Church. Your leaders need your support. For too long, we have been sacrificing the "home team" for the faces and voices in the pews. If leading you, church members, brings them grief rather than joy, it is unprofitable for everyone involved. The Church is not a corporation where stockholders hire and fire their leaders. The Church is a family where God appoints leaders whom we are to encourage, build up, support, and trust. Please make a commitment to pray for your pastors and leaders, to encourage them, admonish them, and provide them the time, energy, finances, and resources to build strong walls in their own homes as they carry the mantle for rebuilding strong walls in the families of their flock.

The Home Front

Notice who is leading the rebuilding effort in Jerusalem: the men. In Nehemiah chapter three, we see the men of the church each leading their own family in the process of rebuilding. Many of them are repairing the very area of the wall in front of their own homes; the men are rebuilding the home front. As the Church (I do not mean the building, but rather the people of God) called to lead in the rebuilding effort, we must recognize that our victories will come by the humble and passionate leadership of our men on the home front. Just as our church leaders have been called to love their wives and disciple their children, so must our men follow their lead. The attack of the enemy on the Christian, and even non-Christian families, in our day may be the most devastating spiritual attack ever waged in the history of the world.

This is not a game, and our families need us, men, to lead them into this rebuilding effort. We must make the home front priority number one, which means we may have to sacrifice in other areas. I have already spent intentional time imploring men to raise the bar when it comes to our personal leadership and walk with the Lord, but I wanted you to see how it applies to the rebuilding effort. I cannot overstate this; men, we are a central piece in the process of rebuilding, and the home front is our most important mission field.

Don't Be a Noble

*"The next section was repaired by the men of Tekoa, **but their nobles would not put their shoulders to the work under their supervisor"*** (Nehemiah 3:5). Did you see that? Right in the middle of this awesome list of priests and families rebuilding the wall, there is this one line about a group called the "nobles." These guys are pompous jerks. Evidently, they are too high up the ladder to join in the rebuilding effort, leaving it to those in lower standings. I heard a great analogy about this once. Always remember this, "the higher you go up the ladder, the smaller the people you are called to serve get, and the more you show your rear end." If somehow you feel the rebuilding of the spiritual walls of our great nation is below you, please get out of the way. Whatever you do with the challenges of these pages, please do not be a "noble."

Division is the Devil

The final thing I want us to see from this scripture is perhaps one of the most understated fallacies in the American church. Notice in the text of the third chapter of Nehemiah how each family is standing next to one another repairing the walls in one accord- UNITY. This indeed is a true miracle. Families align themselves next to each other with one common goal: they are unified in their quest to see the name of the Lord exalted and the walls of their city strong again. There is no dissension in their ranks, no fighting over who is to do what, or bickering over what another family is building. Although the names of the families are listed, it is by the collective effort under one name that they succeed. **Division is a tool of the enemy to keep the Church of God from truly having success in the process of spiritual rebuilding**. Jesus himself once put it this way, "A kingdom divided against itself cannot stand" (Mark 3:24). There is no possible way for me to overstate this point, but at least let me try.

The enemy has waged war on our families, our children, and the next generation of our country, and he is destroying them at a record pace. All the while, we are standing around arguing about whether or not we should use chairs or pews, contemporary worship music or hymns, or whether we should dunk or sprinkle.

We have allowed ourselves to be divided into every kind of denomination and sub-denomination to the point where we are more concerned with the success of our particular kingdom instead of the plight of the vulnerable and broken. Sunday morning in America is the most racially, economically, generationally, and spiritually segregated hour of the week. In battle there are only two sides: our forces and the enemy forces. We need to stop shooting our own and turn our fervor and passion towards destroying the true enemy. My soul yearns to see the Body of Christ be the Body of Christ. We must recognize that until we join hands with true Jesus followers across the aisle, the enemy will continue to have his way with our people. Listen to me; we cannot decide who our brothers and sisters are in the Lord based on worldly standards. Those who have a relationship with God through the risen Jesus are your brothers and sisters in the Lord. I can promise you there will be no last names in Heaven nor a side of town for the Baptist and a different side for the Methodist. Give me a break.

> *As a prisoner for the Lord, then, I urge you to live a life worthy of the calling you have received. Be completely humble and gentle; be patient, bearing with one another in love. **Make every effort to keep the unity of the Spirit through the bond of peace. There is one body and one Spirit—just as you were called to one hope when you were called— one Lord, one faith, one baptism; one God and Father of all, who is over all and through all and in all.*** Ephesians 4:1-6*

We are one, and it is time we start acting like it. We have to throw out the traditions established by man that divide us and begin leading and living according to the Word of God, the Bible. In one accord, we must exalt the name of Jesus above every name because there is no other name given unto men by which we must be saved (Acts 4:12). The stakes are too high and the enemy too clever for us to stand alone. We must learn to put aside the pettiness of our differences to rescue the next generation.

I am not saying that you should align yourself with the cult down the street. We draw our allegiances only with those who have a relationship with Jesus as prescribed by the Word of God; in the same way, we must never destroy allegiances with biblical, Jesus-followers. We need each other more today than ever before. Each family has to do its part for the common good- for the rebuilding of that which the enemy has destroyed. I love this scripture out of I Corinthians twelve because it gives us a great understanding of how the body of Christ should work:

*Now the body is not made up of one part but of many. If the foot should say, "Because I am not a hand, I do not belong to the body," it would not for that reason cease to be part of the body. And if the ear should say, "Because I am not an eye, I do not belong to the body," it would not for that reason cease to be part of the body. If the whole body were an eye, where would the sense of hearing be? If the whole body were an ear, where would the sense of smell be? But in fact God has arranged the parts in the body, every one of them, just as He wanted them to be. If they were all one part, where would the body be? As it is, there are many parts, but one body. The eye cannot say to the hand, "I don't need you!" And the head cannot say to the feet, "I don't need you!" **Now you are the body of Christ, and each one of you is a part of it.** I Corinthians 12:14-21, 27*

Is that not an awesome picture? The eye cannot say to the hand, "I don't need you." Why? Because the eye needs the hand, just as the hand needs the eye. The reason we struggle to rebuild and keep falling prey to the enemy is because we keep saying to other parts of the body, "Hey we don't need you. We can just go down the street and start another church where all the 'feet' can gather." We must begin to realize how desperately we need each other especially when it comes to the discipleship of the next generation. With each division, we become less effective because we dwindle down to single parts of the body trying to accomplish something requiring the full body.

The church of Nehemiah's time understand this principle. They each do their own part- piece by piece they begin to rebuild focusing not on what the "others" are or are not doing, but on what is set before them. What an incredible sight. **The confident, unified body of Christ is an unstoppable force the enemy cannot destroy.** Let me give you a bit of insight into the root of our division so we can repent, or rethink, the way we approach the unification of the body.

Grow Up

You are going to like this. We travel with our young children quite a bit, so a portable DVD player in the car is a necessity. I have seen, or at least listened to, several hundred hours of children's movies. One of my favorites is <u>Finding Nemo</u>. There is a scene where the heart of our division is described to perfection. At one point while Nemo's father is trying with everything in him to rescue his son, he comes across a flock of seagulls. The seagulls are all perched on these poles sticking up out of the water. When they see Nemo's dad and realize he would make a great snack, they begin to fight with one another and say, "mine, mine, mine …" (They sound just like real seagulls when they are trying to eat the sandwich out of your hand down on the boardwalk, and after seeing the movie, I feel certain that "mine" is exactly what they are saying.) Those seagulls always remind me of this scripture found in James:

> *What causes fights and quarrels among you? Don't they come from your desires that battle within you?* ***You want something but don't get it.*** *You kill and covet, but you cannot have what you want. You quarrel*

*and fight. You do not have, because you do not ask
God. When you ask, you do not receive; because you
ask with wrong motives, that you may spend what
you get on your pleasures. James 4:1-3*

Can you hear the seagulls? "Mine, mine, mine...." James
actually tells us in the third chapter of his book that wherever
you find selfish ambition you will find *disorder and every
evil practice.* He is not the only one to warn us of this in the
New Testament. Paul makes it clear in several of his letters
that division in the body is a direct result of selfishness, and
he goes on further to say that it is a direct result of spiritual immaturity (Ephesians 4, Philippians 2). Paul identifies
the blatant truth about the division plaguing our churches.
**The level of disunity in the American church is a direct
result of the lack of spiritual maturity in the American
Christian.** Like two-year-olds fighting over a single toy in a
room with a thousand others, churches fight over members
like there is not a whole world of lost people waiting to
have the gospel change them. We are divided because of our
selfish, immature ambition.

Listen to the words of theologian Matthew Henry about
this very piece of scripture.

*Hereupon, our apostle informs them that the origin of
their wars and fightings was not (as they pretended)
a true zeal for their country, and for the honour of
God, but that their prevailing lusts were the cause of
all. Observe hence, What is sheltered and shrouded
under a specious pretence of zeal for God and religion often comes from men's pride, malice, covetous-
ness, ambition, and revenge.*[16]

We find all sorts of excuses to justify our decisions to
divide. We say we have divided because of a "conflict of

interest" or more spiritually speaking because we have a "*true* passion for Jesus." The truth is, our selfish ambition is dividing the body into unworkable parts. We need to grow up before those growing up after us are left with nothing but dissention and disillusionment in the church. Jesus himself said that He came to the Earth to divide, but let's look at what He divides: the wheat from the chaff, the good fish from the bad fish, the sheep from the goats, and the condemned from the redeemed. He does not want a divided body. He came to unify us under the covering of His blood, and in a prayer to His Father, Jesus himself says, *"May they be brought to complete unity to let the world know that you sent me and have loved them even as you have loved me"* (John 17:23). The world cannot see and understand the love of the Lord or the coming of Jesus to save us if we are not completely unified; the walls cannot be reconstructed until we put aside our selfish ambition and take up one solitary goal- to exalt the Name of Jesus by making disciples of the nations.

We have made a mockery of the cross and the Bride for far too long. Look around. We do not have time for, "mine, mine, mine..." The Galatians struggle with this very same problem, so Paul rebukes them and tells them to refrain from these "acts of the sinful nature." Just turn to Galatians five and read for yourself. You will find selfish ambition, dissensions, and factions listed among their counterparts such as witch-craft, hatred, idolatry, and orgies. If this is not convincing enough, check out Proverbs nineteen verse six. Here, God lists the things He hates, one of them being "a man who stirs up dissension."

God detests the division of the body of Christ. We must not allow the enemy to use us to destroy us. The division of the Church truly crushes my soul because I know we cannot rebuild until we are of one accord. Please pray that God would bring about the unity inside the Church required for us to succeed in repairing the broken walls. Blacks and whites, young and old, rich and poor, Jews and Gentiles: we must be unified under one head- Christ Jesus. Together we must work with one purpose: exalt Him, not us.

Chapter Eighteen

Bricks and Mortar

We have established several things in our time together we recognize as absolutely essential to the perfect process; we have our blueprint, so let's continue with some more practical things that we can do together to further the process of rebuilding. Let's get to some bricks and mortar.

We have already seen that prayer is an essential building block for the resuce effort because the truth remains that we are in desperate need of the God who is able to save to move on our behalf. With our hearts broken and our souls humbled before Him, we must learn to pray. **Prayer is the most powerful unused resource in the American church, in the American family,** and we must learn how to use it in the battle for the souls of our people.

If you are a father, mother, spiritual parent, or guardian of children of any age including those who are grown, make a commitment to pray every single day for the salvation and growth of your children in the Lord. Set aside a time to pray together with your spouse for your marriage, the marriages of your leaders, and your children. Take this time seriously- bow your life and the lives of those you love before a powerful and merciful God and ask Him to come and rescue. Let your prayers be full of admiration and praise for the God of Heaven and Earth, and allow yourself to be open and honest before Him. In repentance, ask God to continue to grow your faith in Him that you might think the way that He thinks and live in accordance with His word. Repent for your nation, and ask God to come and have His way in your homes, your churches, your cities, your government, and your schools. And turn, turn from whatever wicked way your spirit detects in you, turn your family, turn your church, turn and run to the Lord that He may forgive your sins and strengthen your walk with Him.

Combine your prayer with a heart to fast before God on behalf of the next generation- on behalf of your children, your neighbor's children, and the spiritual Orphas God has called you to parent. Ask God to teach you to fast and be willing when He calls you to do so- off with the royal robes and on with the sackcloth. We are after a spiritual break-through, and we recognize through the scripture that fasting combined with humble and faithful prayer turns the ear of the Lord to our cries. Commit to deny yourself earthly conces-sions in order to gain spiritual intercession for the coming generations. Pick a time when you and your spouse can fast together for your children weekly, monthly, or just as the Lord leads. Do not compromise; we have been called to fast before the Lord. Ask God to show you areas of pride in your life and together make a "Declaration of Dependence" to God for your children, their children, the spiritual Orphas, your marriage, your finances, your church leadership, and the breath you have in your lungs. When the people of God get serious on the home front about praying and fasting, the bricks and mortal will spring up like salvation from the ground.

Pastors and church leaders, let me give you a practical application concerning prayer and fasting for your church body. Declare a holy fast and prayer time unto the Lord for the families of your church. Set aside one week, from

Sunday after church to the next Sunday after church and ask your people to fast and pray for the salvation of our children, our marriages, our leaders, and the fame of Jesus. You could even end the fast with a huge victory banquet after church Sunday morning to acknowledge that our God is the great and awesome God. There are several great teaching books on fasting and prayer that you could read in preparation for the time. You can do whatever kind of fast you want as long as the people understand that God exalts the humble but opposes the proud.

Let me take it a step further. Maybe you do no totally agree with the pastor down the street on everything, but you recognize that he is a believer as prescribed by the scripture of God. Call him and invite his church to stand together with you in this week dedicated to fasting and praying on behalf of the next generation. Call your local church association and invite them to join in as well. Call the city council, the school board, the coaching staff at the high school nearby, or the mayor and ask them what they would like you to pray for in their lives and the lives of those they lead. Instead of paying some guy like me to come and preach a "revival" for four nights, simply open the church every evening for families to come and pray together. Invite them to come and receive prayer from your elders or deacons as they lead the way in the fasting and prayer time. Put it on the calendar for next year as well, because the Lord is about to do things in your midst that a million sermons could not invoke.

Get serious about it. Lead the church of God in a prayer of repentance for our nation, for our selfish ambition inside the body, and ask God to send you workers for the fields ripe unto harvest. Pray the prayer of Nehemiah or the repentant and fervent prayer of Daniel. Whatever you do, do not do nothing. Rather than writing an editorial about the school board in the local paper or picketing at the abortion clinic down the street, humble yourself at the feet of the master and ask Him to bring about change in the hearts of people. Ask Him for mercy; do it together with your flock. Let us not merely be hearers of the Word, or even preachers of the Word, but doers of the Word (James 1:22).

Truly, can you imagine joining with your people and even people from other organizations to pray and fast before the Lord for one common purpose? There does not have to be any arguments about which building we should hold the event in, who is preaching, or what sermon they are preaching. It will just be believers standing together in one accord, so the enemy may know you are not going quietly into the night as he destroys our families. I took part in a time like this in my city, and I will never be able to put into words what the Lord did in me, in our churches, in our marriages, and in our city. The effects were far-reaching and not limited to a week. I was standing with men I did not know to pray and fast for our city. I may never meet some of those men, but the unity of the Spirit brought about change in our city. God hears the desperate and humble cries of His people, and He will respond when you call on Him.

If you are layperson and are convinced this is exactly where your church needs to stand, meet with the proper leadership and ask them to pray about doing this together. If they do not feel like it is the direction they need to lead right now, do not supercede them or take issue with their leadership. Pray God would soften their hearts to the position and then trust Him. If they are seeking Him and He is leading that direction, He will move in them. Let Him do it; do not be divisive.

For prayer to be "powerful and effective," it must be done in humility, honesty, and with passion, but most of all, with perseverance and faith. Jesus tells several stories throughout the gospels to give us an understanding how we should pray, but my favorite one is found in Luke. *"Then Jesus told His disciples a parable to show them **that they should always*** *pray and not give up"* (Luke 18:1). Jesus goes on to tell a story about a widow woman who desperately desires for a judge to give her justice concerning someone who wronged her. The judge, however, is not a follower of God, but the woman is persistent, consistent, and does not take "no" for an answer. She simply shows up day after day with her request until the judge finally gives her the justice she desires.

Jesus tells His disciples this is how we should pray: with fervor, persistence, consistency, and faith. If we are going to bend the ear of God for the plight of the next generation, we must be committed to pray this way. Discipleship is not a sprint; it is a marathon, and those who do it well should understand that persistent and fervent prayer is a huge part of the race.

Chapter Nineteen

Follow Me

Jesus started His discipleship ministry with this statement, "Come and follow Me." He is saying to those He calls, "Come and die like Me, come and rise like Me, come and teach like Me, come and heal like Me, come and love like Me, be like Me, train like Me, live like Me, think like Me. Do as you see Me doing, just as I do only what my Father instructs Me." The life of Jesus is the best model we have for the process of discipleship. We must learn to disciple as He did, so I want to walk you through some important keys to discipleship according to the life of Jesus on the Earth. Let me start by clearing up a misunderstanding of the process.

Contrary to popular belief, discipleship is not just a process we start in the life of someone who has recently become a follower of Jesus. Discipleship is often the process that leads people into a relationship with Jesus. Our children, the next generation, follow us as we follow Jesus until the point when they follow Him themselves. If we remember correctly, the twelve men following Jesus for three years are not "Christians" according to the mandate of scripture (Romans 8:9). They do not receive the regeneration of the Holy Spirit until after Jesus ascends into Heaven. They follow

Jesus in an earthly sense, but there is no sign that they are eternal followers until after they are born again spiritually.

It is important to think about discipleship this way because it allows us to see that evangelism is included in the process of discipleship. We start the process of discipleship for our children long before they actually become "Christians." The spiritual Orphas of your neighborhood, church, and city need Jesus; they need the gospel. They need us to evangelize them, but essentially, they need us to evangelize them not just through tracts and one time encounters, but by intentionally leading them to the cross of Jesus.

We must understand that just as discipleship is the process which leads people to the cross, it also equips them to carry on the ministry of Jesus after they come to salvation. Like newborn babies, we must continue to grow them, train them, feed them, protect them, and walk with them until they are ready to do the same for those following them. We are guilty far too often of evangelizing people to the point of conversion and then leaving them on the altar to fend for themselves. Discipleship is not for the lazy. We must continue to equip the saints for the work of the ministry. **Discipleship does not exist without evangelism, but evangelism falls short of the call of God without discipleship.** Let's continue to use Jesus, the Great Teacher, as our example to outline some necessary understandings of discipleship.

Be Connected

You cannot lead others to the cross of Christ or to rebirth in the Spirit of God if you have not personally been to the cross to die and are born again of the Spirit. Simply put- you cannot teach others to walk with Jesus if you are not walking with Jesus. If you are not a Christian, then those following you are not following you towards Him; in fact, it is quite the opposite. Regardless of how "good" a father or mother you are or how much you "love" your children, without a relationship with God through Jesus, the best you can ever offer is the destruction of their spiritual walls. God alone is "good" (Mark 10:18) and He alone is "love" (1 John 4:8). Without Him, we are neither. Void of a relationship with King Jesus, there is no such thing as "good" parents or "loving" families, and there is certainly no such thing as Christ-like discipleship.

So let me ask you this question: Do you have a relationship with King Jesus? Have you died to yourself, been buried with Christ, and raised to a new life in His Spirit? I am not asking if you have been baptized or if you said a prayer when you were seven. Do you have a personal relationship with Jesus? Do you know Him? Do you know how He thinks, how He sounds, how He loves, and how He teaches? For too long in our country we have been making salvation about praying a prayer or signing a membership card, when, in fact, Jesus makes it very clear that salvation is found only in our death and rebirth through the Holy Spirit (John 3:1-21).

No matter how old you are or how many years you spent going to church, I want you to do this for me: Take a moment and be honest before the Lord. Ask Him if you belong to Him. If you do, you will get a resounding "yes" from the Spirit of God living in you. If you do not get that resounding "yes," then I want you to ask God to open your eyes to what salvation in Jesus truly is, and then ask Him for it. Only the Father can draw you to the Son (John 6:43). Call your pastor, your spouse, or a close friend and spend some time in conversation about salvation through Christ. If you do not have anyone that you can talk to, email me. Our website contains my contact information. Whatever you do, do not go another moment without truly seeking your salvation.

"Father I just want to stop and pray this moment
for those who are reading this who do not have a

relationship with You through Jesus. I pray that You would speak to them even now, draw them to Your son, Jesus, and give them new life through the Holy Spirit. Pour out your kindness and grace on them and rescue them. I love you Father, and trust Your sovereignty."

Streams of Life

In John chapter seven, Jesus makes a statement that is truly at the heart of our understanding about the Holy Spirit of God. He says that those of us who are His disciples should have "streams of living water" flowing from within us. Although the Holy Spirit is not given until Jesus ascends into Heaven, the text tells us that this "stream of living water" is truly the Holy Spirit within us. We must understand the importance of this concept when it comes to our discipleship of the next generation. The world is dying of thirst, and we contain the stream of living water they need- He is the Holy Spirit. This is incredible. You and I have within us the very Spirit that raised Jesus from the dead. The Holy Spirit is the lifeline for a lost and dying world. Let's take this thought process one step further through the scriptures. Galatians 5:22-23 tells us exactly what is contained in these streams of living water:

But the fruit of the Spirit is love, joy, peace, patience, kindness, goodness, faithfulness, gentleness, and self-control; against such things there is no law.

These fruits are the "living water" the spiritual Orphas of our day need. They need us to be connected to the Holy Spirit in such a way that we are providing for them the very things they cannot get anywhere else. These are all things the world cannot emulate. The Spirit produces life, while the flesh only produces death. We are imparting the life of God through the fruits of His Spirit to those following us. Each of them is desperate for love, joy, peace, patience, kindness, goodness, faithfulness, gentleness, and self control. Just as a spring feeds a stream, which feeds a river, as God pours these fruits into us through His Spirit, we pour them into those following us. Our discipleship relationships must be characterized by these attributes.

If we are really honest, we know anyone can teach a Sunday school lesson or preach a sermon, but only those who are truly following King Jesus will produce the fruits of the Spirit and change lives. Remember, God is a gardener and so are you. We are to be planting the seeds of these fruits in the next generation. *Love* them without condition, not as the world does based on performance or outward beauty. Share the *joy* of Lord with them and bring *peace* to their lives. Have *patience* with them as He has with you, and overwhelm them with the *kindness* and *goodness* of the Lord that brings repentance. Be *faithful* to your commitment to them, *gentle* in your rebuke, and model for them the *self-control* that only comes from a relationship with the Spirit of God. Wow, that is good.

Let Him Lead

The Holy Spirit is more than the source of spiritual life; He is our guide, our counselor, and the One who brings conviction to the sinner. We must be walking according to the Spirit in order to rightly love our spouses, rear our children, and keep ourselves from the snares of sin. We must have a deep, passionate relationship with Jesus through the Holy Spirit to lead our churches and our cities as the Lord would. As they follow us, so must we follow the lead of the Holy Spirit. Only the Holy Spirit can provide the conviction of sin for a lost and dying world. As He convicts, we stand ready to lead the way to forgiveness, wholeness, and fulfillment in Him. Our understanding even of the scriptures of God is contingent upon interpretation by the Holy Spirit.

Without a strong connection to the Holy Spirit, we have nothing of value to offer the next generation. Our authority, our power, our prophecy, our evangelism, our love, our understanding are all wrapped up in our relationship with the Holy Spirit; without those things, we do not stand a chance in the battle for the souls of our country. Jesus tells us that we are His sheep and recognize His voice (John 10). When was the last time you heard the voice of the Lord for yourself? I do not mean through a sermon, a song, or a book written by a mere man. When was the last time you heard His voice through the work of the Holy Spirit in your life? If this question is difficult to answer, know that you are not alone. Intimacy with the Father through the Holy Spirit requires us to be still, to make time, and to come honestly before Him with regularity. But if we want it, we must do these things.

The Building Gifts

We cannot lead the next generation into an intimate, passionate, true relationship with the Father unless we too are committed to that exact kind of relationship in our own lives. We must produce the fruits of the Spirit, be led and empowered by the Holy Spirit, and we must each learn to use the gifts of the Spirit in order to "build up" the body of Christ (I Corinthians 12). Without the use of the spiritual gifts given by the Holy Spirit, our walls cannot be strong. Each piece must do its part for the overall health of the body. I encourage you to spend some time before the Lord, in His Word, with His Spirit asking Him to pour out His spiritual gifts that you might learn exactly how to use them for building up the Body of Christ.

Let me say one more thing about this. You cannot determine your spiritual gifts with an aptitude survey as so many churches are employing these days. The gifts are given by the Spirit as He determines, not based on personality traits or personal areas of excellence. Just because you are a banker does not qualify you to serve on the finance committee. (Truth is, this kind of thinking is part of the problem all together.) Your spiritual gifts are determined by the Spirit, and the only way to know which gift or gifts you have and how to use them is by being in intimate relationship with the Holy Spirit. There are no surveys for that. It will take time, prayer, maybe even fasting, and a willingness to use whatever the Lord gives you to build up His Body. In the same manner as discipleship, there are no short cuts.

Be Compelled

We disciple because we love the Lord; we love those He has called us to love because He first loved us (1 John 4:19). Discipleship is incredibly difficult, and those who do it out of the wrong motivation will fail. Let me give you an example. If you are teaching Sunday school, working with the youth, serving as a deacon, singing in the choir, or serving on a committee based on any motivation other than your love for Jesus and your love for others, you will fail. Love, however, never fails (I Corinthians 13).

You can always tell which teachers, committee members, or even pastors are serving based on something other than love. If they serve based on guilt or shame, they whine about the smallest things and seldom teach sin as sin. If they serve out of selfish ambition, they always compete for the biggest class, and tell you how many folks showed up this week, making sure you know how hard they work. They will always be objects of division in one way or another. (This is the group I can find myself in if I am not careful.) If they serve out of duty or religious obligation, they possess no passion or connectivity with those they are called to teach; they just do their duty and move on.

But when people serve based on a deep love for the name of God and the people of God, they are always willing to go the extra mile without the slightest fanfare. The people they serve would give their life for them without hesitation. We must always be willing to check our motivation at the door. If we find ourselves being motivated by anything other than a love for the glory of God and for those He has called us to, it may be time to submit our "ministry" before the Lord until our hearts are rightly compelled to love and serve as Jesus did.

Be Concise

Jesus chose His disciples, they did not choose Him. In the same way, God chose your children for you, and as much as people like to think that their two and half children, the small dog, and the white picket fence are their own planning, God is still the author of life. If you have children, then God has already given you a great clue as to whom He has chosen for you to disciple. Now there may be more spiritual Orphas out there whom God has ordained for you, but you know for sure the ones living in your house are chosen by God to learn from you. If you do not disciple them rightly, God may choose to bring them a spiritual parent from somewhere else, but you are ultimately responsible for their spiritual up bringing. Start there- before you set off to cross the globe making disciples, make sure you have crossed the hall in your own home.

Having said that, God is also in charge of choosing for you those, outside of your earthly family, whom He wants you to spiritually parent or foster. Jesus was concise in the process of discipleship. Jesus, God in human form, only had twelve close disciples, so what makes us think we can rightly instruct hundreds? Yes, He spent much time healing the masses and teaching thousands in church, but the majority of His intentional discipleship was spent on twelve guys, even one He knew would betray Him in the end. He was concise, and although Jesus called each of these guys to follow Him, according to the scripture, God ordained them for Jesus (John 17:6). God wants to choose disciples for you. Twelve is not a magic number, but it is a great example of the precision God requires of us when it comes to making disciples.

Here is the problem. The harvest is plentiful, but the laborers are few. If your heart beats out of your chest with a passion to disciple the next generation, you can quickly and easily get overwhelmed with the sheer numbers of spiritual Orphas who exist- which is exactly why you and I are having this conversation. We need a generation of workers to stand up and make themselves available for this process; each piece doing its part. Our pastors are not called to disciple thousands of church members. They may be called to lead thousands of people inside their church organizations, but they are called to lead them through the training of other leaders in the church.

Jesus gives us the perfect example of this. He teaches thousands with every crowd who follows Him, but in the first chapter of the book of Acts we see that after His ascension into Heaven the church only numbers about 120, and of that group, we can only identify a small number of close disciples of Jesus. He is concise in His approach to true discipleship just as we should be. He remains reliant upon the leading of His father for exactly what they would become, just as we should be.

We start here. Whether you are a Sunday school teacher, a pastor, or just a solid follower of the Lord Jesus, I want you to begin to pray and ask God to show you exactly who He has chosen for you to disciple. Start with your children and then be open to hear from the Lord concerning the spiritual Orphas in desperate need of your love and guidance. Then get ready because He may be preparing you to take a leap of faith that will lead to the incredible restoration of a soul.

When He places that person on your heart begin to actively seek Him as to exactly how you should approach the process. I like to try and do it the way that Jesus did.

When God stirs my heart for someone He wants me to actively invest in, I just call and tell them that I want to them to *"follow me."* I tell them that I feel like God has placed them on my heart in a special way, and I offer myself, my resources, and my family to them completely. Time and again those whom I approach this way are completely over-whelmed that the God of the universe cares enough about them to send someone into their life to train them in righ-teousness. The children of the next generation are dying for someone to single them out. They are dying for someone to invest solely in them; they are desperate for someone to acknowledge their value with a commitment of any kind. They are in need of being chosen, just like we were. They need to feel wanted and desired. You will be amazed at the hunger many of them have to walk rightly with the Lord.

Think about it this way. You are a fifteen year old girl living with mom and step-dad number two. You go to church with a thousand people, a school with 1500 other students, and both mom and step-dad work 40 hour weeks. You truly desire to walk with the Lord but do not know how. Then one day, an older friend of a friend singles you out and asks you to hang out at his house after school. You are blown away that he would take any interest in you at all. Why? Because no one else ever has. One year later, you find your-self sitting at the abortion clinic, head in hands, trying to make sense of exactly where you went wrong. That is not just a story I conjured up, it is a story written day after day in our country.

Let's flip the script and look at what might happen when those called to make disciples take their call seriously. Same girl, but this time the person showing interest is a thirty year old mother from your church telling you how she feels called of God to invest in you. She invites you to come over to her house and eat supper with her family once a week. A year of care from this spiritual big sister and her family, you are now walking closely with the Lord. At school one day, you notice a seventh grade girl who looks much like you did at that age. God moves in your heart to do for her what has been done for you. So, just as you have seen modeled, you invite her to youth group on Wednesday night, so you can start the process of investing in her. The power of concise discipleship is that it continues to reproduce itself. When we allow God to make choices for us, we honor Him, and He honors us. One disciple at a time, the walls are rebuilt. It is beautiful, and I am smiling just thinking about it.

Chapter Twenty

Follow Me Some More

Be Committed

Jesus trained the same twelve guys for three years. Can you imagine spending every waking moment with the same twelve guys for three years? I hope so because parenting children takes even longer than that. Sometimes, I look at my wife and we ask one another, "How long are these children going to be living in our house?" Discipleship takes an incredibly insane amount of commitment. Discipleship is often messy and hard, and it can be incredibly disappointing when those who follow us chose to walk in the ways of the world, but we must trust God for the increase. *I planted the seed, Apollos watered it, but God made it grow (1Corinthians 3:6).*

Ultimately, we must trust God for the results, but we must also be committed to process of discipleship out of our own obedience and love for the Lord. Jesus committed everything He had to the process of seeing these guys truly get it, and it was not until after some of them saw the holes in His resurrected body that they got it. He spent countless hours teaching them, training them, testing them, feeding them, saving them, rebuking them, and loving on them. Jesus did not meet with them once a week over coffee to discuss theology, Jesus did life with them. He trained them for three years so when the time came, they would be ready to take up the mantle of the gospel of His death and resurrection. There were many times, when it seemed as if they would never understand the truth of His kingdom, but He pressed on with them. Like a father to his children, He protected them, disciplined them, and prepared them for the road ahead. He did it by example, in power, and with grace. He committed to stay with them through the doubt, mistakes, and even through their denial of Him. This is the kind of discipleship the next generation is in desperate need of.

One of the major issues facing the students and children filling our schools and coffee shops today is in the area of commitment. They do not understand it because many of them have never seen it modeled. The marriage commitment has become a side bet, the commitment to sexual purity has become like Big Foot- everyone has heard that it exists but we have no evidence of it, and the commitment to faith in Jesus has become a last option for the weak-minded. As a generation, we need to redeem the faith in commitment by simply modeling it for the world to see. We must make a commitment to the rebuilding of the walls and no matter the cost, stand firm in our resolve until commitment means something again in the eyes of those who follow us. Jesus made a promise that was no doubt incredibly difficult to keep as the flesh was being torn from His body for the sins of those holding the whip. *Let us fix our eyes on Jesus, the author and perfecter of our faith, who for the **joy set before Him** endured the cross, scorning its shame, and sat down at the right hand of the throne of God (Hebrews 12:2).*

The willingness of Jesus to endure the cross is the exact example we must follow with those following us. We must make a commitment to stand in the face of adversity, inside the process of discipleship, and endure the cost as the joy set before us. The spiritual Orphas of our day need to know that though the world may fall into the sea, we will not abandoned our commitment to their spiritual well being. For many of the children in the next generation, all they know for certain is that sooner rather than later, those called to lead them will abandoned them. Think about it. Parents divorce, youth pastors move on, coaches get fired for not winning, teachers are overwhelmed to the point where they have to quit in order to save their own lives, so who is left holding the bag? You got it, Generation Next. This is why it is imperative when we feel called by God to disciple someone that we commit to the process until the Lord comes. In your lifetime you may only truly disciple a few children, but it may take your entire lifetime to do it rightly. When you do it rightly, they will do it rightly, and eventually, the fruits of your labor are too many to count.

Spare Room

A few years ago, my wife and I met a young girl named Krista in a small town not far from where we live. Eventually, we talked her into going on a mission trip with us where, for the first time, we learned her story. Her mother fell dead of a drug-related incident when Krista was just ten years old, and she never truly knew her father. She was an orphan in more than the physical sense. It was not long after the mission trip when we learned she had become pregnant and was being kicked out of the family with whom she was living. My wife, Kimberly, was heartbroken and began to pray about the baby she was carrying and about how we could minister to Krista.

We had some friends from the church who were unable to have their own children and had previously adopted a daughter. Kimberly began to feel like the Lord was leading her to mention the family to Krista in hopes she might desire to give up the baby for adoption. After praying about it, we both decided we should at least mention it to her. As time progressed, Krista came to the conclusion that the Lord would indeed have her give up the baby to this couple. At mid-semester her senior year of high school, Krista moved in with the family who was going to be taking the baby. We felt great. "Look at us, we have really made an impact in this young girl's life."

About two months later, we got a phone call from the soon to be adoptive parents asking us if Krista could move in with us until the baby was born so they could prepare for the birth of the baby in a way that would honor Krista's feelings. What? We had done our part, right? Wrong. God was calling us to a deeper commitment to Krista's life. We thought about it and decided she could move in until after the baby was born. Then she would be off to college, so it was no big deal. Krista finished high school and began preparing for the birth of the baby and college all at the same time. One morning she walked into my bedroom and said, "I think I am in labor." Kimberly rushed her to the hospital and several hours later, I was there to see one of the most incredible things I have ever witnessed- something that changed my life.

Krista and the baby were doing well. The adoptive parents were waiting in the hall to see their new baby when Krista called us into the room. She was holding the baby boy as we all entered the room. She asked me to pray; I did not know what to say, but I prayed anyway. Then she took the baby boy and kissed him and quietly called to the adoptive mother standing nearby. With incredible resolve and grace, she handed the baby to the adoptive mom. I fell apart right there. I had never seen anything like it, but I knew exactly what it meant for that baby boy- he was going to have strong walls around his life.

Walking out into the hallway and looking at my own children, I also knew what it meant for the adoptive parents- a lifetime of commitment to training their son in righteousness. They were committing to feed, nourish, and provide for this baby that was not even theirs by birth; they were making a commitment that has no end on this Earth. They did not ask to meet with the baby once a week and feed him, or even to send him money from time to time. They committed themselves to his life, to raising him up. God was wrecking my soul with this understanding, but He was far from through with me.

After the baby was born, Krista enrolled in a college several hours away, and then God stretched us out once again. She had no car to go to college and no way to get one. We had one; it belonged to my wife. So God began to impress upon us that we should give my wife's car to her. (I hear you guys out there saying, "yeah his wife's car.") I reasoned that it was older, paid off, and would make a good college car. Besides, Kimberly needed a new car anyway, so we gave her car to Krista. She had the car three weeks before she hit a deer and totaled it. We collected the insurance from it and bought her a small compact car to get back and forth to school. Discipleship was starting to cost us in more than one way.

When the time came, we took a Saturday, loaded up all of Krista's belongings, and moved her into her dorm. "Man, had we really gone the extra mile or what?" I kept thinking we were going to get some kind of "Christians of the Year" award or something. For that year at school, Kim spoke with Krista on occasion, and we moved on with our busy lives. As summer approached, Krista called and asked if she could visit with us about her summer plans. She informed us she would not be returning to that college because she did not pass enough classes to re-enroll. She informed us she had been into drugs and several other things during the school year, and although her school was totally paid for, she did not spend much time actually going to class.

Kimberly and I did not know what to do. God was about to teach us an incredible lesson about the spiritual adoption process- about the commitment to discipleship. One day as I was sitting with the Lord and praying about the entire situation involving Krista, the Lord clearly spoke to me. Here is a paraphrase of what He said, "Kevin, you failed her. I did not send her to you so you could buy her a car and send her off to school. I sent her so you could disciple her, and you did not. You did not provide her with the spiritual tools she needs to walk with Me out there. I want her to be a part of your family; I want you to train her in the ways of righteousness. I want you to commit to her so she might see how I have committed to you. I want you to teach her about unconditional love by loving her the way I have loved you. I want her to follow you and your bride to the point where she can follow Me. Take her back into your home and this time, do it out of love for Me and for her, not out of a need to revered by men."

Kimberly got the same kind of message from the Lord. We owed her an apology; she gave us one as well, and God got the glory. She is now in her second year of nursing school, and the Lord is transforming her life. God was not asking us to invest only our resources; He was imploring us to follow His example by giving of our lives. Krista is one of the best investments we have ever made as a family, and one day she will get the opportunity to pass it along to those God calls to follow her. Discipleship requires commitment.

All across the cities of America, there are countless Christian families with *spare room* in their homes and in their lives. Many of you have raised godly children who are now on their own, but you have those two extra bedrooms and some spare time. There is no retiring from making disciples. I want you to think about this: What if we filled all of the *spare room* in the homes of strong, righteous disciple-makers with "Kristas" and other spiritual Orphas? What if

220

the church took discipleship to the place where God intended it to happen- inside the home, inside the family? Can you imagine the eternal impact this kind of commitment to the Great Commission could have on the next generation of America?

What I am asking may seem a bit over the top, but desperate times call for godly measures. Pastors and church leaders, let's really take this thing to another level by asking the people of the church who are strong Jesus followers to join us in filling the *spare rooms* of our homes. Opening our lives, our resources, and our homes to the spiritual Orphas existing in our land, and allowing God to use us to truly stand in the gap for the broken and vulnerable, will rebuild walls unimaginable.

The family is the mechanism for discipleship, and the home is the place where children learn to become men and women of faith. All I am asking is that we be willing and actively seek God about the possibilities. Begin to pray, and make your home and your resources available for whomever God would have you disciple. **Sunday morning is a great time to make an investment in the lives of others, but Monday morning is when they need it the most.** There are countless college students and even many high school students who are in need of a family, in need of spiritual fathers and spiritual mothers. As difficult as it may be, fostering children from broken homes is an incredible way to invest in the salvation of the next generation. I cannot think of a single act on this Earth that honors God more than spiritually fostering a child in need. God's very character is described in this way:

*"A father to the fatherless, a defender of widows, is God in His holy dwelling. **God sets the lonely in families...**" Psalms 68:5-6*

Buying Back God's Children

I think maybe the most beautiful picture we have on this planet of the incredible love of the Lord can be seen through adoption. The Bible clearly teaches us that although we were spiritually orphaned by our sin, God who is rich in mercy adopted us through the blood of His only son into His eternal family (Ephesians 1:5). Standing there in the hospital that day, watching that young adoptive mother take this baby into her arms for first time, knowing the incredible commitment ahead of her, I could see it. God loves adoption. He loves when His people make a commitment to a child of the next generation in need of not only physical parents but spiritual ones. He loves it, because it is His very heartbeat. The redemption of children, the protecting of the vulnerable, and the discipling of the nations are the very heartbeat of God. Adoption is a picture of who God is, and for many of us, it may be the most incredible opportunity to rebuild the spiritual walls of the next generation.

I will never forget a conversation I had with a young man who has become one of the most popular Christian songwriters of our time about this very subject. I was aware that he and his wife had just adopted a baby girl, so I was curious as to why. They were young and healthy, and he never mentioned that they could not have their own children. When the opportunity presented itself, I asked him why they adopted. His answer changed my heart on the subject and caused me to rethink, to repent. He said their motivation was simple; they were just buying back God's children from the world. Adoption done with this motivation is redemption in its purest form. If you have not considered adoption, I want you to open your heart to God's leading in this way.

Recently, my pastor and his wife made an overwhelming commitment to the discipleship of "Generation Next" when they set out to adopt three children from Africa. The Lord chose to put those children under the care of another family, but the heart of our church is forever changed. Of all the incredible things our church has learned from our pastor and his family, this act of obedience is the most incredible kind of leadership we have experienced. My prayer is that their obedience opens the doors to the *spare room* in the lives of many of the people of our church and city. When we ask God to chose for us those He has called us to lead, we need to be open to whatever that call might look like. God calls us to obey Him and rescue them. Truly, my heart is alive thinking and dreaming about the impact the Church of God could have with a little bit of *spare room* and a true commitment to the future.

For many of you, God is not calling you to bring someone into your lives in this way, but I can tell you for sure that when God calls you to disciple someone, He does not mean just over coffee once a month. The investment you make in the spirituality of the next generation will be the most incredible investment possible and will require an incredible amount of commitment. I simply want you to pray about how God would have you commit to the process of discipleship in the life of someone who desperately needs it. Perhaps God is calling you to start by being involved with the church youth group or children's ministry. Maybe you can find the time to coach a little league team or join the pastor on some home visits. Whatever the case, my hope is that you will become serious about asking God whom He has called you to disciple and about the commitment this process requires. As you agree to open your life to discipleship, God will show you those with whom He desires for you to go the extra mile. When He does, contact them and tell them you want to make a commitment to invest in their lives. Then make the commitment.

Be Consistent

Commitment over time validates the truth of our commitment. One of the major gripes of young people everywhere is that as a generation, adults are people who say one thing and do another. We have already discussed how this affects a world of people who are skeptical at best, and the results are much the same for the coming generations. We must follow the example given by Jesus; He was consistent. He was consistent in His teaching, in His love for others, in His passion for the broken, and in His pursuit of salvation for all mankind. In a world where the cultural landscape is changing every moment of every day and young people are dealing with a brand new attack from the enemy at every turn, Jesus has not changed. He is resolved and eternal, and has called us to be people from that same mold. We must always be growing in the Lord, but the consistency of our character will stand beyond whatever attack the enemy employs and whatever direction the culture dictates. The people who follow us as disciples should be able to depend on the consistency of our character, our love, and our commitment to the glory of God and His purpose in their lives.

Be Caring

One of the greatest men I know, a man who mentored me in the ministry and taught me much about commitment, character, grace, and discipleship, once shared with me a proverb which I have seen come true continually in ministry to students everywhere. He said that students, children, and people of all kinds "will not care how much you know until they know how much you care." I know it has been said thousands of times, but that makes it no less true. As a matter of fact, it is more true in the culture our young people live in today than ever before. They are desperate for those of us inside the church to simply care for them. This is more than just an emotional connection; it is a set of actions on our part. Think about it this way. If you ask me to care for your seven year old for a week, you would expect me to do several things. You would expect me to feed, clothe, protect, bathe, and even discipline him. Discipleship takes on this very nature in the life of someone God has called us to care for, and it is this kind of caring that brings about some of the most awesome spiritual breakthroughs. We are making a commitment to care for someone spiritually, physically, and even emotionally.

One of the things we have discovered with the children's orphanage we have in Kenya is that more than anything, the children simply need someone to care for them. Once they understand that we are there to feed and clothe them and that our motives are pure, they quickly open their hearts to the Jesus we serve. Once we have proven we are there to care for them, they are most interested in not just what we know, but whom. His name is Jesus, and He is awesome. Let me also say this: Training requires that we love them enough to discipline them. God disciplines those He loves (Hebrew 12:6). Show me a parent who does not discipline their children, and I will show you a child who does not feel loved. Are you caring for the next generation? Because the moment you begin caring for them, they will start following you. When they do, it is your chance to lead them to the cross and the empty tomb of King Jesus.

Chapter Twenty-One

Candid and Crazy

Be Candid

I repeatedly hear one request from the current generation of young people about the adult generation inside the church: they want us to be real. I want you to think about this one for a second. Look at the most popular kind of television programming in our country over the past decade- reality television. They are after the truth. Even today with a reality TV show about everything from cooking to catching crab in Alaska, this generation wants to continue taking it further with internet sites like Facebook and YouTube. These sites are so popular with the young people of America because they perceive them to be candid and real. Much of the disinterest with the "church" we are getting from this culture is based on the fact that they see the "church" as everything but candid. They view it as "fake."

They are after the truth, and the time is now for us to remove the Sunday morning mask and share with them the truth of Jesus- uncut, unadulterated, and candid. While we skirt around certain hot bed topics, Oprah is tackling their questions head on with a bunch of psychobabble and false teachings about God. Oprah is a liar; Jesus is the truth

(Romans 3:4). We must be willing to present them with the Bible just as it is written. They do not need the picture version where Jesus is handsome and surrounded by white doves; they know that is not real. **They need an ugly, bloody cross where the Savior of all mankind who had *no beauty or majesty to attract us to Him* was stripped naked and beaten beyond human recognition for our sin.**

We must tell them the truth about everything from life and death, to sin, Hell, and Heaven. We must be people of the truth and learn to hate anything that represents the lies we keep passing down from generation to generation. Church membership, baptism, or being the son of a pastor cannot save you. God is more concerned about your holiness than He is your happiness. Sexual immorality is exactly that- immoral. Everyone is not a winner. You cannot show up and expect a prize. There is no such thing as a "participation trophy." Those who have a relationship with Jesus according to the Word of God win in the end, those who do not are "disqualified from the race." These are the truths of God's Word. We do not have to agree with them for them to be true. I realize the truth can often seem harsh or unloving, but it is love not lies that covers a multitude of sin- my sin, your sin. For too long, we have been allowing "little" lies to work their way into the fabric of our children, and blaming it on "culture." We are crippling them. We must throw out the standards of culture and impose upon them the Truth of the Jesus Culture.

Let me give you a broad example that always helps me "rethink." Santa Clause is dead; Jesus is alive. Don't freak out; just give me a chance to explain. Think about it- from the time our children are little, we tell them about this magical guy named Santa Clause who has flying reindeer and elves. We tell them he is immortal. We explain that he is all-knowing and will judge whether they have been good or bad. We tell them he is kind and giving. We put his picture up on our front doors and sing songs about him. We even go so far as to have our children write letters to him or go in person to make requests (pray) to him.

Then we go to great lengths to trick (deceive) our children into believing that he brings them the great gifts they receive at CHRISTmas time. At the same time, we tell them about this magical man named Jesus, who could walk on water, make the blind see, and who loves children. He too is immortal and all-knowing. We put His picture up on our front doors and sing songs about Him. Children are encouraged to pray and bring their requests to Him also. The only problem is, He does not bring them anything at CHRISTmas time. Santa, not Jesus, gets the credit for bringing good things; even though the Bible teaches *"every good and perfect gift comes from above" (James 1:17)*. Then one day, we tell them that the whole Santa Clause story is a lie, but the Jesus story is true. Without a thought, we then expect them to simply offer their lives to Him.

Can you see the problem? Santa Clause is a lie; Jesus is the truth. Like the idols the people of Israel trust, Santa cannot bring salvation to all mankind. We cannot expect the Lord to honor even what we believe are "little" lies in the lives of those He has called us to lead (II Corinthians 4:2). We should never offer our time, energy, or worship to anything that is not Jesus, nor should we teach the next generation to do so. If we plant lies, we reap lies. The culture has convinced us, even as Christians, that it is "o.k." because it such a small thing; it is not a small thing to the great and jealous God who created us (Deuteronomy 4:24). Worship Jesus, love Jesus, sing about Jesus, tell stories about Jesus, and honor only Him- He is the truth. Our children need the truth.

Let me give you a couple of examples from my own experience about how desperate the next generation is for the candid truth. About a month ago, I was walking with an older adult sponsor at camp when a young man, probably around twenty years old, approached us and asked me if I would give him some advice. I said, "Sure, what's up?" He then proceeded to ask me, "If I masturbate without lusting, is it still a sin or just part of my physiology?" You should have seen the look on the face of the youth sponsor. I answered his question very forthrightly and even included a testimony about having asked myself that question before. He went away satisfied with the truth and hopefully, to sin no more. That subject was not a part of any of the teachings he heard from me at camp, but he was in search of the candid truth.

A couple of years ago, I was sitting at a lunch table with a group of ninth grade girls. We were just chatting about school and so forth when one of the young girls in the group spoke up. She said, "O.K. Kevin, enough of the small talk. We have a question for you." I said, "Go for it," and all at once, they leaned in towards the table as if they were about to get the winning numbers to the lottery. They posed this question, "We want to know how far is too far when it comes to being physical with boys?" I answered the question, not by my opinion, but based on the scripture. Although several of them did not like the truth about it, they all agreed that is was the truth. The next week they had a complete list of questions for me. They found a place they could get the candid truth and they were hungry for it.

Those following us need the truth about life and about walking with Jesus in this crazy world. They are in search of answers to the questions the world is posing to them, and we are allowing the enemy to be the only voice in their world. For too long, we have been allowing our seeker-sensitivity to water down the naked truth about sin, death, and Hell, but what is it we think the seekers are seeking? They are seeking the candid truth, and if there ever were a man on the planet not afraid to speak the truth, it was Jesus. His candor and willingness to take on the tough questions, even the toughest adversaries, brought everyone from the sick and broken to the greatest teachers of His day.

I had a student recently tell me that they would rather hang out with someone who was openly homosexual than the crowd of snooty, "holier than thou" Christians from the local church. When I asked, "Why?" he simply answered, "Because at least they are real." Now, his perspectives may be a little distorted by the fact that he is lost, but it does not change the fact that those who follow us need to be able to see us for what we truly are. They need to know that we too are depraved, evil sinners saved by the grace of Jesus. They need to able to identify with our brokenness in order to identify with the Savior who set us free from sin and death.

Jesus came to be a our Great High Priest, but what makes Him believable is that He humbled Himself as a man and faced the same temptations we all face. He is not an unapproachable God, and even though He remained sinless while on Earth, His willingness to expose Himself to the plight of humanity gives us great comfort. God made Himself candid in our midst. He came down off the stage and shared in the discomforts and pains of human life. He was real. You could touch Him and see Him; He felt real pain. Like many of us, He too was betrayed. He had promises broken, people close to Him died, and He cared about people to the point of tears. He was not handsome; He felt ridicule and was rejected by men. He was not esteemed (Isaiah 53). Ultimately, He showed us the very reality of His humanity when, in the garden before His father, He pleaded with God to find another way to save humankind. Then He honored and obeyed His father, even though His flesh did not want to endure the shame and pain of the cross. Jesus was real.

We must come down from the stage and invest in the lives of the next generation with candor and honesty, or before long we will be standing onstage in front of any empty auditorium. I am amazed when students take the time to send us emails and letters simply thanking us for being "real." I have learned why it is such a big deal: Many men and women have stood before them in a nice suit, with perfect hair, and an All-American smile. They profess to be one thing, but as it turns out, they are something totally different.

If by some stretch of the imagination we think the young people of our churches do not know the difference sitting in the audience, we are sadly mistaken. If you have children, you will understand this line of thinking. Children have a way of seeing beyond the mask to the heart of people. Of all the people in the world who see you in your most candid moments, your children are at the top of the list. If you do not want the world to know it, be careful what you say in front of them because odds are at the most inopportune time, they will repeat it.

When you invest whole-heartedly in someone, they should have this same insight into your life. They must know and understand your struggles, your hang-ups, your weaknesses, and your true heart's desire to be holy before the Lord. Here is a great litmus test: if someone who is following you could live with you for two weeks, would they learn anything different about your character than what they have seen inside the walls of the church? Think about it; when we take discipleship out of the confines of the church building and put it back into the homes of Christian men and women, it will not only benefit those we are training, it will also push us to reevaluate our own candid character.

Think about these twelve guys who were with Jesus all day, everyday. Do you ever wish you could have been able to see Jesus in everyday life, not on the preaching tour or just inside the church, but in everyday life? We have; He is exactly the same. Are you? I often struggle with this, but it is the process of and reaction to the struggle those following us need to be able to identify. They must be able to see us fall in order to know how to get up. They must be able to see us offend, in order to know how to apologize. They must see us get offended, in order to know how to forgive. They must be able to see us accomplish great things, in order to know how to give God all the glory.

Do you remember the story about the tax collector and the Pharisee in Luke eighteen? The Pharisee goes up the temple to pray and says, "God, I thank you that I am not like all these other sinners, especially this tax collector. I fast twice a week and give a tenth of all I get." The first thing I think about this guy is that he is probably a pompous jerk, and I would not want to spend a second under his leadership. Would you? Then the tax collector takes the stage and cannot bring himself to even look toward the heavens. In a moment of true candor and humility, he simply admits he is a sinner and asks God to have mercy on him. Now this is a guy that I can relate to.

One last note for all of you who are about to go and share every sin of your past, present, and the ones you are planning for the future with those learning from you: Being transparent is not about taking pride in your sin or making it a banner over your life. I run into those guys who give their testimony about the sin they once lived in as if it were their prize possession, somehow believing that sharing it with the world makes it o.k. We should never glorify sin in any way, but those who follow us must be aware of our sin and our eminent struggle with the temptations of the enemy, so that when we defeat him, they will know it is because of the Jesus in us.

Here is a candid principal we must all live by: If you mess up, fess up. I wish I had a dollar for all the times I have had to go to my children or other children who are following me to confess my sin and ask their forgiveness. The truth sets them free; it sets me free. One of the most discouraging things we see when dealing with children and young people is the overwhelming amount of them who believe they are in some way responsible for their parents divorce. Dad and mom never stepped up to tell them the truth, and the enemy seized the opportunity to fill their head with lies. He is liar, and he has come to kill, steal, and destroy our homes, our marriages, and our children. Please be honest with those following you. Be the grown up. You are not protecting them by keeping them from the truth; you are crippling them for the road ahead. When we confess our sins to those following us, we are setting an example for them about how to approach God and about how to forgive as He has forgiven. The simple truth will set them free; it will set you free.

Be a Little Bit Crazy

It is our true passion, fervor, and zealous love for Jesus those following us must experience in order to rightly know how to worship, adore, and exalt His Name. I have been to more than my share of church services which from all appearances seem like funeral services, and I am sick and tired of it. Now don't jump off the caravan in assuming I am alluding to the style of worship used by some churches; I am not talking about worship styles at all. I am talking about the dead hearts of the so-called worshipers. Should we not be a little bit crazy about a God who sent His perfect Son to rescue our undeserving souls from an eternity in Hell? Should we not lose it a bit when we consider the brutal sacrifice Jesus endured to save us? As evil sinners saved by grace, should not the passion of our praise be equal to the pain of His sacrifice?

This is not about personality or styles of music; those are just excuses we so often use for being ungrateful and uninspired worshippers of the living King. Are you kidding me? I grew up on the some of the most powerful words of songs ever written. Words like, "Because He lives, I can face tomorrow, because He lives all fear is gone, because I know He holds the future and life is worth the living just because He lives." Did you hear that? Life is worth the living because we do not worship a dead God, so we should live it like crazy. Our Savior is alive, well, and living in the hearts of His people. He lives in us. He saved us even though we hated Him. The passion with which we praise Him should have nothing to do with song style or personality. He is worthy of our praise, our adoration, our very lives, and there is a generation standing in the street waiting for a passionate people whom they can follow.

The generation coming after us is described as a generation passionate about nothing. They are in need of leaders and trainers who are head over heels in love with the God they serve, and who live lives of passionate service to the King who saved them. What kind of picture are we painting of our God and our salvation for those He has called to follow us? We need to get over the structure of worship, the style of worship, the length of worship, and get back to the reason for worship. He is Jesus, and He is worthy of our insanity. Listen, you do not have to be loud and animated to be a herald for King Jesus, but you should have a deep-rooted passion for His Name that should be clear to those who follow you.

Passion in contagious and so is the plague. Which of those are we carrying? As a key for discipleship, those who follow us must be able recognize our deep love for Jesus and our overwhelming sense of gratitude for His sacrifice. They are waiting to be inspired by something real, something worth being passionate about. We need to make a big deal out of King Jesus, so they might learn that He is in fact a big deal. It is not enough to raise our hands and dance a holy dance on Sunday morning (although that would be cool); we must invite those following us to see and understand from our lives that we are a little bit crazy about Jesus. They must be able to see our passion for Him lived out in our jobs, homes, relationships, conversation, music, tragedies, and in our victories.

I know you know someone who is passionate about something in particular; take that guy in your office who is overly passionate about golf. You know, the one who has the membership to the golf course with his own cart and the latest, greatest equipment. He is always reading <u>Golf Digest</u> and telling you about the adjustments he is making to his swing. He "fasts" from lunch on Tuesdays so he can leave the office early to meet the Five O'clock group. He is constantly inviting you to go play with him and his other psycho, golf buddies. He uses phrases like "well that is about par," in every other sentence, and he keeps a small photo of Tiger Woods next to the family portrait on his desk.

Can you see it? Hey, I love a good round of golf, but if we are going to be truly passionate about something, should it not be about the Savior who died and rose for us? We should be "that guy" who is always doing ministry somewhere. We are always reading our Bible and making adjustments to our attitude. We don't eat lunch on Tuesdays because we are fasting for the spiritual growth of our children. We are always using words like "grace" and "mercy" and singing songs about God's goodness. Those following us should never have a question about our love and passion for Jesus. Ask yourself these questions. Does the world know about my infatuation with Jesus? Do they know that I am a fanatical Jesus worshiper? Then ask yourself the really hard one: Am I infatuated with Jesus? Can we expect those we are training to adore a God we barely mention? No. As the generation leading a generation, we must set an example of the greatness of our King by the passion we exhibit for His Name, His Church, and His call to commission. This gets me pretty excited. I was a horrible sinner before my Jesus rescued me, and in a million days on this Earth, I could never exalt Him enough to repay Him for what He did for me. I am in love with Jesus, and I want those following me to have no doubt about that.

Those following us must be able to identify not only our passion for Jesus, but also our faith in Him. We must allow them to be a part of our faith walk with Jesus. Often, the things God calls us to be a part of are not "logical' or even safe, but we are called to be people who follow Jesus no matter the consequences. We are called to walk by faith, not by sight. Those following us can learn a great deal about how to trust the Lord based on His faithfulness in our lives. Let them in on your struggle to trust God, the insurmountable odds you are facing, and on the faithfulness of the victory you find in Jesus. When God calls you to adopt a child, spend three months doing medical work in Africa, or give up cable television to raise money for a local orphanage, crazy things. Let them see you trust Him for it all, and when He proves Himself faithful once again, give Him the glory. You must be a little bit crazy to truly follow the Lord on this planet, but until we do, we know for sure that the walls cannot be rebuilt. Lives lived by faith are an incredible adventure far beyond the mundane, moderate, measured, and religious lives so many young people equate to Christianity. Generation Next is desperate for modern-day examples of the radical, passionate, dangerous lives of the followers of Jesus so vividly described in scripture. Those guys were definitely a little bit crazy. We should be too.

Chapter Twenty-Two

Consumed by His Word

I saved this one for last because I believe it to be the most important aspect in the process of rebuilding the spiritual walls.

After Nehemiah and the Jews finish rebuilding the physical walls of Jerusalem, they set out on a journey to rebuild their nation spiritually. They do so by simply getting back to the teachings of the Word of God. Nehemiah chapter eight tells us that after the walls are rebuilt, Nehemiah calls all the Jews together to listen to the reading of the Word of God. Ezra reads the Old Testament laws to them from daybreak until noon everyday for a week. It creates an incredible revival in the hearts of people as they begin to repent, worship, and bow down before the God of the Bible.

As leaders called to rightly lead the coming generations into passionate relationship with the God of the universe, the most important thing we can offer them is the written, inspired, inerrant, living Word of God. It is the most powerful tool we have in the battle for the souls of the next generation. There is no equal to its ability to penetrate the hardest of hearts, and there is no lie of the enemy it cannot expose. The Word of God is, and will always be, the centerpiece of the process of discipleship. It contains not just the words of

God but the very character and person of Jesus. It is alive and actively drawing sinners to repentance, the broken to wholeness, the sick to healing, the people of God to glory, and satan to account for his actions.

> *For the word of God is living and active. Sharper than any double-edged sword, it penetrates even to dividing soul and spirit, joints and marrow; it judges the thoughts and attitudes of the heart. Nothing in all creation is hidden from God's sight. Everything is uncovered and laid bare before the eyes of Him to whom we must give account. Hebrews 4:12-13*

The Word of God is the standard for all things that call themselves truth, and the guide for everyone who calls himself a follower of the Truth. **The Word of God is not something we merely study academically; it is, in fact, something we encounter supernaturally**. It is Jesus, and we are in desperate need of it right now in our families, churches, cities, and in the lives of the broken and wayward children of America.

I grew up in a house with three younger sisters and one bathroom. I know, let's just say there is a very stunted bush in our backyard and some neighbors who were glad I moved away. My mom had this routine for us in the mornings that I thought was pretty awesome. She would wake all three girls up first and when they finished using the bathroom she would come in and say, "The girls are out, the bathroom is all yours." (I know. I was spoiled rotten.) On most days after mom woke the girls up, she would begin the process of making us all muffins. I absolutely love blueberry muffins but evidently the making of muffins requires every single pan in the kitchen, because it always sounded like mom was preparing for World War Three.

As if that was not enough there was the issue of the oven. My dad is "Mr. Fix It," and sometimes he holds onto an appliance a little too long if you know what I mean- that was the case with our oven. Dad "reworked" the oven door because it was not shutting properly. If you happened to get your hand caught in the closing door, you put yourself in danger of losing a finger or two. Anyway, my mom would bang around for a while and then like clockwork, she put the muffins in the oven and the sound of the "reworked" door slamming shut resonated through the house. Then there would be a much welcomed silence, a silence only inter- rupted by a single sound- the very distinct sound of the pages of my mom's Bible turning. My mom would sit at the kitchen table every morning and pour over the Word of God.

Some time later, after I left the house, I asked my mother about her daily Bible reading, and she said something that changed my life. I do not remember her exact words but this is what I heard, "Son, I am not merely reading the Bible, I am meeting with Jesus. He is breathing on me, teaching me, inspiring me, loving on me, and preparing me to be the wife and mother He called me to be." My mother's father was a preacher for sixty years. His name was JR Williams. He served in several small churches in many small towns during those years. He had no seminary training and often had other jobs just to make a living for his family, but he was one of the greatest Bible scholars the world has never known. He read the Bible from front to back some 400 times, and on the day he died, I stood next to him and read him the Psalms. I started them and he finished them. He loved the Word of God, and it loved him. You see, my mother was simply living out the spiritual legacy of her father and passing that legacy on to me. I have never received a greater gift and will never give one greater to those who follow me than a deep passion for the Word of God.

The single greatest tool we have as re-builders is the Word of God, but for far too many of us, it is the one tool we use the least. We are a people who call ourselves followers of the God of the Bible, but we are not a people who can say we truly know the God of the Bible because an overwhelming majority of American Christians would have to confess they have never even read it all the way through. In the days of Jesus, Jewish children went to school under a rabbi in a room often adjacent to the synagogue. They studied the Torah, or the Law- the first five books of the Old Testament. During their time of study, it was not uncommon for children as young as twelve or thirteen years old to memorize the entire Torah. They memorized Genesis, Exodus, Leviticus, Numbers, and Deuteronomy, and they did it without possessing their own copy.

Those who carried this kind of discipline often went on to become talmidid- or disciples of a rabbi. They professed to follow the God of the Bible, and they meant it. This is not meant to shame anyone, but consider this: you and I can get the Bible in any language, with any kind of cover, with small print and large print, in dozens of translations, or even on compact disc, yet many of us cannot quote a verse from any five books of the Bible.

We have confessed to the world and to the children who are following us that we love and adore the God of the Bible, but we have neglected our responsibility to truly know the God of the Bible. Listen, this is not some religious brow-beating that ends in everyone giving an excuse and me feeling like a jerk; this is the truth, a scary and understated truth. As repairers of the broken walls, we must change this. I need you to understand that there are plenty of men and women out there who have studied the Bible endlessly and their knowledge has done nothing but puff them up (1 Corinthians 8:1). I do not like those kinds of people very much. They annoy me just as Paul said they would; they are like a resounding gong or a clanging symbol, having all the knowledge in the world but no love (1 Corinthians 13). I am not petitioning for that, but what I am petitioning for are followers of Jesus who are willing to encounter Him through the Bible not just for personal growth, but for the reestablishing of the spiritual walls. If we are going to sound the alarm and run recklessly into the world to save the spiritual Orphas of our land, we must take along with us the Sword of the Spirit, the living Word of God.

Wield the Sword

As you look at the story of rebuilding in the book of Nehemiah, you will find that several things take place as the reconstruction of the wall of Jerusalem gets under way. In chapter four, the re-builders face great opposition to the point that Nehemiah has to take some action. Here is what he does:

> *I stationed some of the people behind the lowest points of the wall at the exposed places, posting them by families, with their swords, spears and bows. After I looked things over, I stood up and said to the nobles, the officials and the rest of the people, "Don't be afraid of them. Remember the Lord, who is great and awesome, and fight for your brothers, your sons and your daughters, your wives and your homes." Nehemiah 4:13-14*

Nehemiah calls for the men to arm themselves against the enemy, and later in chapter four, we see an incredible picture of the tenacity and commitment of the re-builders when Nehemiah tells them to carry with them a sword in one hand and to rebuild with the other. They are literally protecting their families with the sword while they rebuild the walls of the city. This is such an awesome picture of exactly what God has called you and me to be about today, but unlike the men and women of Nehemiah's time, the sword we carry is much different. The apostle Paul puts our war and our weapons into the proper perspective for us in Ephesians. I am going to include this entire scripture so you can see straight from the Word of God the call for us and the importance of our weapons.

> *Finally, be strong in the Lord and in His mighty power. Put on the full armor of God so that you can take your stand against the devil's schemes.* ***For our struggle is not against flesh and blood, but against the rulers, against the authorities, against the powers of this dark world and against the spiritual forces of evil in the heavenly realms.*** *Therefore put on the full armor of God, so that when the day of evil comes, you may be able to stand your ground, and after you have done everything, to stand. Stand firm then, with the belt of truth buckled around your waist, with the breastplate of righteousness in place, and with your feet fitted with the readiness that comes from the gospel of peace. In addition to all this, take up the shield of faith, with which you can extinguish all the flaming arrows of the evil one. Take the helmet of salvation and **the sword of the Spirit, which is the word of God.** And pray in the Spirit on all occasions with all kinds of prayers and requests. With this in mind, be alert and always keep on praying for all the saints. Ephesians 6:10-18*

There is a battle raging in the heavens for the souls of our children, and we are called to stand firm. We are called to wield a weapon in the defense of our families, our churches, our marriages, and our cities. That weapon is the sword of the Spirit- the Word of the living God. The Bible is much more than an academic book to be studied by mere men; it is the chosen weapon of a people called to protect and disciple the nations. A single scripture, enhanced by the power of the Holy Spirit, at the exact moment of temptation, is able to quickly expose the lie and give us the strength to stand in the face of satan. There is no substitute for the training up of the next generation- not this book or any other book. "The B- I-B-L-E, yes that's the book for me. I stand alone on the Word of God, the B-I-B-L-E." These are the words of a Sunday school song I learned as a child, but it has taken me many years to recognize the power and truth of its message.

The Recipe for Victory

My whole life growing up, at the beginning of what seemed like every school year, my mom would hand me and the girls each a 3X5 recipe card with a scripture on it that she felt like the Lord wanted us to remember during that year. *(In those days, 3X5 index note cards we refereed to as recipe cards because they were used to write cooking recipes on.)* My sophomore year in college, I decided I really did not want to be the "good child" anymore, so I thought I would try my hand at being my own god. I simply disregarded the teaching of my childhood and spent some time in the world. Well, because you mothers out there have some kind of sin sonar, my mom was fully aware that I was not living according to the Word of God, nor was I spending any time in it. (We normally don't when we feel certain that it is going to cramp our style.)

One day I went to the mailbox expecting to find the usual-nothing, when I found a card there from my mother. Inside the envelope there was a single 3X5 recipe card with a single scripture written on it. I will never forget it. The scripture was Psalm 119:9 and it said, *"How can a young man keep his way pure? By living according to Your Word."* It was signed, "Mom and Dad, we love you N/M." I quickly put it away and tried to escape the obvious truth and power of the scripture for my life, but when I returned to the mailbox a week later, there were six new envelopes all including 3X5 recipe cards with scriptures written in my mom's handwriting and the same signature, "Mom and Dad, we love you N/M." For what seemed like an entire semester, my mom sent me the Word of God in the mail every single day. She was keenly aware of something that you and I must come to understand-The wayward children of the next generation do not need our opinions or well thought-out discipleship books; they need the Word of God.

> *But as for you, continue in what you have learned and have become convinced of, because you know those from whom you learned it, and* **how from infancy you have known the holy Scriptures,** *which are able to make you wise for salvation through faith in Christ Jesus.* **All Scripture is God-breathed and is useful for teaching, rebuking, correcting and training in righteousness, so that the man of God may be thoroughly equipped for every good work.** *II Timothy 3:14-17*

My mother knew and trusted the power of the Word of God. She taught me the scripture from the time I was an infant, and trained me to respect and honor the teachings of the Bible. She was counting on the living Word of God, Jesus, to penetrate my hard heart. I did not last long. I caved under the influence of the Word and repented. Years later I asked my mom about that semester and she simply said, "I figured you were not reading your Bible everyday, so I thought I would help you along." I also asked her about the odd ending to the signature on each card: "We love you, N/M." She told me that the N/M stood for "No Matter What" and in a classic example of spiritual legacy, to this day when

I put my children to bed, I say to them, "I love you, no matter what." Not only did my mother have knowledge about the Word of God, she truly lived it out in my life. She is called to love me without condition just as Jesus loved her; just as you and I are called to love those following us.

The Seed

I want you to think back to the gardening principle we talked about earlier; we are planters, and what we plant will grow. I want you to understand this as it applies to the Word of God. My mother spent much time planting in me when I was a child. She planted the Word of God because Jesus tells us in Luke that the Word of God is the seed that you and I are to be planting in the lives of those we are called to disciple. She planted the Word of God in me with passion and consistency, and today even in the writing of this book, she is reaping the Word of God as a spiritual legacy because I am planting it in the lives of those who follow me. We must get back to teaching and training disciples in the Word of God, *so that the man of God may be thoroughly equipped for every good work.*

Stands Forever

Let me give you one more incredible reason for us to learn and teach the Word of God to those called to follow us. This scripture is incredible.

*For you have been born again, not of perishable seed, but of imperishable, through the living and enduring word of God. For, "All men are like grass, and all their glory is like the flowers of the field; the grass withers and the flowers fall, **but the word of the Lord stands forever."** 1 Peter 1:23-25*

The truth is that one day my mother will no longer be here; just as her father went on to be with Jesus, so will she. But the Word of God that he planted in her, which she planted in me, will endure forever. Thousands upon thousands of preachers have come and gone, but the Word of God is still standing. Thousand upon thousands of books have been written, read, and forgotten about, but the Bible is still supreme. I recognize that if the legacy I leave my children is not God's Word, then it is truly worthless; likewise, if we choose to leave our children and the spiritual Orphas of our day a legacy of deep passion and reliance on the Word of God, then we truly accomplish something for eternity. We not only rebuilt the spiritual walls around our heirs, we also give them the eternal tools to keep those walls strong until the day when the Word Himself returns to take His bride home.

There is no need in our country that exceeds the need for the prominence of the Word of God. It is, it has always been, it will always be the Enduring Truth, the Light shining brightly in the darkness, and the very Bread of Life. Let us be people of the Word, creating children of the Word, so that from generation to generation the walls can stand firm under the attack of the enemy. There are many people across our great nation who have lost all hope for the walls to be strong again, but our hope is in the Lord, and we stand upon the Word of God, the B-I-B-L-E.

Chapter Twenty-Three

Elders to Infants

As we get ready to wrap up our journey, I want to take the opportunity to share with you some real life ideas I think can help set the tone for the perfect process in our churches and homes. How can we see the process of intense lifestyle discipleship take shape in our churches and homes? Let's talk about an idea for our churches that I like to call "Elders to Infants."

Step one: Identify men who are worthy of respect.

Most churches have either an elder board or a deacon body of some kind. If we are following the protocol of scripture, then the men who serve in these groups should be men who are worthy of respect, whose homes are in order, who produce the fruits of the Spirit, and who have a passion for and understanding of the Word of God. If those are not the kind of men making up the elder or deacon board in your church, my first suggestion would be to remove them from their position as a stated leader until their lives do agree with the scripture in I Timothy chapter three. Then, begin to pray that God raise up those kind of men in your church because the discipleship of the next generation will only be as effective as those men.

Step two: Pastor or pastors training elders (three to six months)

As a pastor or church leader, you should already be in the habit of meeting with and training the men of your elder or deacon board on a regular basis. They should be familiar with your family, with your passion for Jesus, with your deep roots in the Word of God, and with your vision for the people God has given you to lead. If this is not the case, then start by taking an intentional time of at least three months to bridge the gap between you and the men you have been called to disciple. Have them in your home, share with them, out of a candid heart, your desire to grow them and to see them grow the families of your church. Take them through a Bible study of some kind. Do whatever it takes to invest in their lives inside and outside the church. Bring the idea of the week of fasting and prayer before them and secure their support and their leadership. It is imperative as the leader of those men, you have a personal Christ-like relationship with them where you are accountable to one another, and you are highly active in teaching and encouraging each other.

You are not a C.E.O. and they are not your corporate board of directors. You are a shepherd called to do whatever it takes to lead, protect, feed, teach, and care for the families of your flock. (Always start with your own family.) So take three months, or whatever time table you may need, and establish this relationship with your mighty men of valor because the very things you pour into them is going to be required of them to pour into others. Remember the Church is designed to be a river, not a lake. **Discipleship that does not produce discipleship is not discipleship at all.** The next section of the book will give you some great discipleship ideas you can employ during this time with your elders. Over the course of three months, lay out a plan that will allow your elders to minister to every age group in the church over the course of one year, starting with the week of fasting and prayer. Here is how it might look.

Step three: Elders training the next generation (three months)

During the last month of your intentional discipleship time, implore each elder or deacon to pray and ask God to give each of them **six** other men they can disciple in the same way you have invested in them. Let's do it by generations. As a general rule, most elder boards are made up of men beyond their forties, not always the case, but you can account for that. Have your elders chose six men in their thirties or even forties they feel God would have them intentionally invest in. For the next three months, your elders disciple these men in the exact ways you have modeled for them. They have them in their homes, teach them how to rightly divide the Word of Truth (even doing the same Bible study they just completed with you), model for them a Godly marriage, and inspire them to be re-builders of their families and of the spiritual Orphas.

Remember, it is not the method that is paramount; it is the blueprint of Nehemiah and the commission of God that should be the focus. They must garnish a relationship with these men akin to a father and a son, or a craftsman to his apprentice. It will take time, energy, effort, resources, and intentionality, as all good training does, but they must understand that they are investing in these men so these men can turn around and invest in the next generation. It cannot be done meeting once a month over coffee; it is going to take a greater commitment than that.

Step four: Paying it forward for the next generation (three months)

During the last month of this three month process, the elders are to challenge each of their six men to pray about

three men of the next generation, possibly college age guys or even high school students, who they feel the Lord would have them invest in. For the next three months, they repeat what they have learned from the elders of the church, making a commitment just as they have seen modeled and remembering the rebuilding tools that are vital to the spiritual livelihood of the next generation. These men take these three months to train their three mighty men of valor with the understanding that their next step is to invest what they have learned into the lives of those following them.

Step five: Back to junior high (three months)

During the last month of their training, have each of the three men begin to pray and ask God to impress upon them **one** young man, possibly someone in junior high, who they can disciple for the next three months. Just as they have seen modeled they make a commitment to the spiritual welfare of one young man and impress the same passion for the Word of God, the same love for King Jesus, and the same personal relationship that extends outside the walls of the church. With each generation affected by the teachings of your leadership, the language may change a bit, the approach may look a little different, but the process will be powerful and effective.

Step six: Changing diapers, changing lives

During the last month of the training process for the junior high boys, their trainers present them with one simple challenge. Challenge these young men to commit to spending one month every Sunday or Wednesday volunteering their time in the children's ministry of the church. Allow them to be teacher's aides, share their testimony, or simply work in the nursery one day each week for one month. You will obviously have to coordinate with the children's ministry, but if the one in your church is like mine, they can always use the extra help. Can you see it? We are not just training; we are training the next generation for the purpose of training the next generation. We are teaching each generation their responsibility to the next one. By example, we are securing the future of the spiritual walls for generations to come. We are teaching our children how to follow us, how to follow Jesus, and how to lead the next generation to do the same.

Over the course of one year or even a year and a half, depending on how you structure the time, your elders will have had a direct impact on the children's ministry of your church, and they did it without ever spending time in the nursery. This is called discipleship and it is a pattern that God intends for us to employ from one generation to the next, establishing a strong future for the Church. Here is what is important to remember: After their three months together, each tier continues to spend time investing in those God has put under them so the accountability is strong and the personal relationships continue to grow. Not only is each group growing in the Lord based on the things they have learned, they are also learning to invest in the next generation.

Just for grins consider this: if the discipleship process is modeled as above, and you start with twelve elders, then you will directly impact 516 men over the course of one to two years (not including the young men of the children's ministry). Can you imagine? I realize that to get this kind of commitment from this many men will require a true miracle of God, but that is the point. We are asking God for miracles, and we are training those who follow us to be men of great conviction and commitment. We are becoming repairers of the broken walls.

Remember that each of the men in the process do not have to be Christians or members of your "church." Can you imagine how salvation could spring up from the ground if we choose to truly walk out the call of God on our lives? Obviously, if someone does not become a believer during the three month process of discipleship, we cannot ask them to lead someone else, but what if they do? Can you think of a better understanding of God's call to commission than helping them see the value in being a part of rebuilding the next generation? The numbers, the lengths of time, and the idiosyncrasies of the process are not paramount- the process, however, is. Take the second year and encourage the women of the church to follow the exact same pattern, or do it with families, couples, or even just from your high school to your junior high. The important thing to remember is that we are trying to teach the process of discipleship in such way that it regenerates itself. Discipleship done correctly always produces more discipleship. The apostle Paul gives us this exact principle in his instructions to his spiritual son Timothy. I love this.

*You then, my son, be strong in the grace that is in Christ Jesus. And the things you have heard me say in the presence of many witnesses **entrust to reliable men who will also be qualified to teach others.** 2 Tim. 2:1-2*

There it is. Paul teaches Timothy, his adopted spiritual son, Timothy teaches reliable men, and those men teach the next generation- From the pastor, to his elders, and on to the next generation. What an incredible picture God has given us. In the closing chapters I am going to give you some more specific ideas when it comes to living out this process in everyday life. These are all elements that you can incorporate in the Elders to Infants model. I am excited just thinking about this.

Chapter Twenty-Four

Everyday Ideas

Have Them in Your Home

Whether you are committing to fill the "spare room" or just have your disciples around you on a regular basis, so much of the effectiveness of discipleship happens in the home. They need to see you interact with your wife and children; they are looking for a model different from what they have seen in the world. Invite them over to sit down for a family meal, let them come by and use your washing machine, or any other excuse you can think of. Let them help prepare the meal, or help you with some work on your car. Just involve them. Get out your checkbook and pay some bills while they are there. They may need a lesson in how to honor God with their finances, or a lesson in how to get a job. Put them to work and model for them the work ethic that you desire the next generation of Americans to have.

Involve them. When I get a teenager in my home these days, one of the first things I do is ask them to help with my computer; most of them can. Ask them questions about everything from sports and politics to marriage and Jesus. Always include Jesus. Invest in them the time and energy the Lord has invested in you. Train them. You would not believe how many young people do not know how to change a flat tire or do laundry. Every second they are "on the roof" with you is an opportunity to train them in the Lord, and your home is the perfect place for that.

***Elders to Infants note: Do this at least once a week if you can. Set up a night during the week to have them over for anything; just get them in your home.*

Take Them with You

In our ministry we call this principle, "Get in the van," because we take college students with us for different ministry opportunities. Jesus did it by walking up to a couple of guys who were working one day and said, "Hey, you guys come with me." They had no clue where they were going, and I am not sure that mattered because they were going with Jesus. Remember our text out Deuteronomy 6:7:

*You shall teach them diligently to your sons and shall talk of them **when you sit in your house and when you walk by the way** and when you lie down and when you rise up.*

We see both of these principles outlined here. Have them in your home so you can invest in them there, but also "when you walk by the way." Take them with you wherever it is that you are going. Invite them to a ballgame, to ride alongside you as you visit people in the hospital, to a local soup kitchen, to coach your son's soccer team, or to praise band practice. People often spell love, T-I-M-E, and so often it does not really matter what that time is spent doing as long as they are with you and you are investing in them. Maybe you are a runner or a fisherman. Maybe you love to cook, play golf, or quilt- I don't know, but whatever you are doing as you "walk by the way," take them with you. They will learn to do life in Jesus by watching you learn to do life in Jesus.

For so many of our children and spiritual Orphas, the only models they have seen are worldly. This is where we change that. How do you treat a woman? How do you be a woman? How do you interact with the lost or treat the waitress at a restaurant? All of these things are teaching opportunities God has ordained for us in the training of the next generation, and they carry much more weight with those following us when they are done outside the walls of the church. Jesus took His guys for a really long walk and as they "walked by the way" they learned everything they needed to know.

***Elders to Infants note: At least once a month, commit to taking your guys with you somewhere. It could be all at once; it could be one at a time. This may be a little harder for the high school guys but they can do it with the man they are following and the young man following them. Help them make the process go.*

Let Them Try, Let Them Fail, and Teach Them How to Try Again

Sometimes in reading the gospels about Jesus and His group of merry men, you just have to laugh. For instance, there is a story in Mark nine that is just funny. The situation is not funny, but what happens with the disciples is hilarious. There is man who has a son who is possessed by a demon (that part is not funny). The man brings his son to the disciples, but they are not able to drive out the demon. When Jesus shows up, it only takes Him a few seconds to rid the boy of the evil spirit. After they get alone with Jesus, the disciples question Him about why they could not drive out the demon to which He answers, "Oh yeah, this kind of demon only comes out with prayer and fasting." This part is not recorded, but you have to know the disciples were thinking, "Yeah thanks Jesus. You could have mentioned that before we were over there looking like idiots trying to drive out this demon." I mean think about it; what was that scene like after several of them had tried and failed? They were arguing that maybe Peter was not saying the right word or that John was not holding his hands right.

These guys are just men following Jesus, but Jesus is training them for the work of the ministry. He could have cast the demon out before they failed, but they would not have learned anything. With our children or those God has called us to train, we must at some point say to them, "Hey why don't you try it this time." We must give them a chance to be a part of the process, or the process itself is useless. You do not train an all-star quarterback or world-class ballerina by simply showing them how to do it; you must let them try and fail and be there to teach them how to try again. If you have been cooking for a while, then it may not be a difficult task for you; however, if you have ever tried teaching your children to cook, that is a whole different story. It is going to take much more time, patience, and cleanup if you decide to teach them by letting them try and fail. In the end though, they will learn more thoroughly how to accomplish the task.

Discipleship works just as Jesus modeled it. It is about training and then empowering the next generation. As a youth pastor, I was allowed very minimal time in the schools where so many of the students we were trying to reach were for eight hours a day, but I had a secret weapon- Discipleship. I trained my high school guys and my high school girls to minister to those younger than them, to be spiritual leaders. Here is one of the huge flaws in the way we do church ministry: We want our young people to be seen but not heard. We are challenging them to lead, to set an example, and to be strong in the Word of God, but we never allow them any opportunity to do just that inside of the church. For instance, how many search committees, finance committees, or other leadership groups in the church contain teenage men and women? Not too many. They need to be empowered to lead and trained to lead rightly.

Look at it this way, the young people of America are like motorboats whose motors never stop running, and who often have no rudder whatsoever. They have lots of energy and zeal, but many of them have not been disciplined under the teachings of the scripture. Our job as their trainers is not to make them shut off their engines; our job is to be their rudder until the time in which they can trust God for their own direction. We are not to quench their spirit; we are to empower and train them. A group of teenagers rightly trained and empowered by the church can cause more change in a day than most church leaders can in a year. Let them try, and if they fail, teach them how to try again.

***Elders to Infants note: Find a way to get them involved and hang in there with them when they start the process for the next group. Teach them to teach and then help them accomplish it.*

Be a Resource for Them

Take the time with those God has called to follow you to be a resource for any area of their life where there is a need you can fill. For instance, if I need an appliance fixed, or anything for that matter, the best resource I have in the world is my dad. If I have a problem or an issue with my children that I cannot figure out, the best resource for me is "super mom," my mom. If I have a financial question, one of my resources is an accountant who has invested time and energy in me. You get the picture, but unlike me, many of the young people filling our schools and colleges do not have a list of people who have invested in them as a resource. One of the things we try to do as a ministry is to be a resource for college students who need a job. We have contacts with several businesses in town we know are run by Christian men and women. It is perfect match. The students get a job working with people who will invest spiritually in them, and the businesses benefit because they know that if they have a problem with one of our students, they can call us and we can step back in as part of the spiritual training process to be a rudder for them. These students need men and women who will be a resource for them, and inside the church, we have a network of incredible people with the resources to help them accomplish their goals.

****Elders to Infants note: Be intentional about making your resources available to those following you. Find out what they need and help them accomplish their goals.*

Bless Them for No Reason

Many times in my life, the Lord has blessed me to the point that it is just too much. His overwhelming kindness to me brings about great repentance in my soul. As a great example of the Lord's blessing, we too should be a blessing those who follow us; not just because they have done something good, but because God has done something good. Be a river of blessings to those who God has given you. As He blesses you, you turn around and bless your disciples. Out of the blue, give them a call and buy them lunch. For no reason, take your daughter on a date and treat her like the queen of the world; that is called training. Randomly leave a gift for them, not because they deserve it, but because God gave you the ultimate gift when you certainly did not deserve it. Be a blessing to them, and in doing so, you will teach them how to be a blessing to those who follow them. My children and I often sit around and ask God how we can bless someone today who is in need of a blessing. Sometimes, we will go get mom a Dr. Pepper or call up someone and sing them a silly song, but every time we do it, I know they are learning something about the incredible heart of the Lord.

***Elders to Infants note: At least once a month figure out a way to bless those following you for no reason. Then help them be a blessing to those following them when they start the process for the next generation. Set an example- they will follow it.

The Recipe Card

We have talked at length about the importance of the Word of God in the process of rebuilding the spiritual walls, and I shared with you the story of how my mom used a 3x5 recipe card to change my life. In whatever way we have to do it, we must actively put the Word of God before the children of the next generation. Here are a couple of ways.

Speak it. Go back to the scripture from Deuteronomy. It implores us to talk about the Word of God always. Let the Word of God become the language you use all day everyday. This does not mean you have to start every sentence with, "And God said," but I would challenge you to use the language of the Bible in everything you do. Let it be the overflow of your heart and the guide for all decisions you make, especially with those you are training. For instance, when your children, or those you are training, have done something deserving punishment, but you feel like you should take it easy on them this time, take it easy on them. Describe your leniency as "mercy," and explain to them that God has given you great mercy, and you are extending that same mercy to them. My mom would always tell us as children that "bad company corrupts good morals." I remember thinking that must have been something Confucius or someone like that said. You can imagine my surprise when years later, I read that exact verse, not out of the Farmers Almanac, but straight from I Corinthians 15:33. Use the language of the Bible, so when they begin to encounter the Word for themselves, they will see and understand that your training manual for them was, in fact, the only viable one.

Write it on the doorframes of your house and your gates. Take those 3x5 recipe cards out and write down scripture. Put them in places where you know they will see them. On the bathroom mirror, in their car, on the front door of your house; we simply need to get the Word in front of them, and it will do the rest. I do not know if you have heard, but there is a new form of communication taking over the world- text messaging. It is awesome. Texting makes up a huge percentage of the communication young people in our country are involved in on an everyday basis, so text the Word of God. Ask God to give you a scripture He feels they need to see today and text it to them. You can use texting to send the Word of God from one side of the world to another in a matter of seconds. Take the time once a week, or even once a day, and text scripture to all those you are training. Email is another form of cyber language we can use to get the Word of God in front of the next generation; just do not be that guy who sends an email saying that if you do not forward it to ten people then you hate God, and a piano will fall on you today.

Let me share one more story with you about the power of the Word of God in the life of a young man who grew up in my youth group. He was from a fantastic home and had potential dripping off of him, but somewhere along the way, he bought a lie. He eventually got caught up in drugs and several other pleasures of the world, and his parents were beside themselves. They did everything they could: kicked him out, took him back, loved him without condition enough to discipline him, and protected him the best they knew how. One day his mother and I were talking about his wayward state; she was asking me for some advice, some encourage-ment. I shared with her the same story I shared with you about my mother and the 3x5 recipe cards. She agreed that the Word of God was a powerful tool and decided to begin

262

the process of using those recipe cards to put the Word before her son.

She sent them in the mail, put them in the bathroom, in his car, and everywhere else tape would stick. She and her husband prayed that the Word would penetrate his hardened heart. I was there the night his parents threw him a huge "Prodigal Son" party. I listened to him as he apologized and repented for his sin, and then I asked him, "What made the difference? What brought you home? What caused you to break?" He said, "Come in here and I will show you." Together we walked into his bathroom, he pulled open the top drawer in his cabinet, and there was a stack of 3x5 recipe cards with the scriptures of God written in his mom's handwriting. We both stood there with tears in our eyes- those 3X5 recipe cards rescued us both from ourselves.

The Word of God is a powerful tool for the rebuilding of spiritual walls. It is the recipe for the restoration we are so desperately in need of today. If I were you, I would buy a huge stack of those recipe cards- they make great rebuilding tools.

****Elders to Infants note: If you do know how to text message, learn. You can send a text of the scriptures everyday to those following you, and a card at least once a month. Fill your home and your language with the truth of God's Word. It will not return void. Isaiah 55:11*

Section Eight

The Reward

Chapter Twenty-Five

Repairer of Broken Walls

So the wall was completed on the twenty-fifth of Elul, in fifty-two days. When all our enemies heard about this, all the surrounding nations were afraid and lost their self-confidence because they realized that this work had been done with the help of our God. Nehemiah 6:15-16

It took Nehemiah and the families of Jerusalem fifty-two days to rebuild the walls of Jerusalem, and when the enemies of God heard about the miracle He had done on behalf of His people, they crumbled in fear. God did something in their nation that could not be attributed to any man, organization, or government; only He could receive the glory. You see, rebuilding the walls for the coming generations in America is about Him, His glory, His move, and His name; only He can accomplish it. I believe, with every fiber of my being, that we are due for a miracle like this right now in our country. I am pleading with everyone who calls themselves followers of the great and awesome God to take up the mantle of restoring our children, our families, our churches, our spiritual Orphas, and our cities. I am pleading for us to take urgent action.

Let us come together and declare a holy fast unto the Lord and pray in humility and brokenness to the God of the universe; let us repent and turn from our wicked ways that He might hear us and rescue our land. Then you and I can get about the business of training up the next generation in righteousness, so when they are old, they will not depart from it; rather, they will train up the next generation. The people of Nehemiah's day faced great opposition and hardships in repairing the broken wall of Jerusalem, just as we will everyday in a culture that does not welcome the things of God. But one look in the other room where my children lay sleeping, and I know for certain it is well worth it.

I am so grateful you have walked with me through this entire process, but I am pleading with you to make this the first chapter in the story of our restoration. One more time, let me encourage those who are already standing in the gap on the wall- our pastors, teachers, coaches, stepparents, mom, and dads, together we can see the walls rebuilt. Moms- do not give up praying for your children. Husbands- do not give up in making your marriage strong. Youth pastors- do not give up trying to reach the least of these. Pastors- please do not give up caring for the sheep of your flock including those in your own house. Oh Church, the beautiful Bride of Christ, the hope of the world- do not give up training the next generation to walk with Jesus. Raise high the Name of Jesus, honor the commission of the great and awesome God, and rescue the spiritual Orphas.

Here is our blueprint one last time. **Recognize** the devastation, assume **Responsibility**, **Remember** the great and awesome God who is able to save us, **Repent** in humility and brokenness, **Risk** it all to see results, and **Rebuild** the broken walls. As God honored these steps by His people in the days of Nehemiah, He will honor them in us. Our **Reward** will be waiting for us in eternity- generations of strong, righteous disciples of King Jesus.

Here we are Lord. We are ready to rebuild. For your name's sake and for our children and their children, we say "yes." May You be glorified and exalted in all we do. We want to be called the "Repairer of the Broken Walls."

Then you will call, and the LORD will answer; you will cry for help, and He will say: Here am I. "If you do away with the yoke of oppression, with the pointing finger and malicious talk, if you spend yourselves in behalf of the hungry and satisfy the needs of the oppressed, then your light will rise in the darkness, and your night will become like the noonday. The LORD will guide you always; He will satisfy your needs in a sun-scorched land and will strengthen your frame. You will be like a well-watered garden, like a spring whose waters never fail. Your people will rebuild the ancient ruins and will raise up the age-old foundations; you will be called

Repairer of Broken Walls.

Isaiah 58:9-12

Appendix

Note: All Bibliographic entries are given in the order they appear in the book according to their superscript. This is intended to make finding the source information less complex as you read the book.

1   Fredrikson-Bass, Jenni Annabel Kannabus. "HIV and Aids in Africa." <u>AVERTing HIV and AIDS</u>. 18 Nov. 2008. Avert.org. <http://www.avert.org/aafrica.htm>.

2   Jones, RK et al. "Abortion in the United States: Incidence and Access to Services." <u>Perspectives on Sexual Health</u> 40 (2008): 6-16.

3   United States Census Bureau. "Household Income Rises, Poverty Rate Declines, Number Uninsured Up." <u>United States Census Bureau News</u>. Washington: 28 Aug 2007.

4   Abma, JC et al. "Teenagers in the United States: Sexual Activity, Contraceptive Use, and Childbearing." <u>Vital and Health Statistics</u> 23 (2004): 24.

5   Associated Press. "Almost 4 in 10 U.S. Children Born Out of Wedlock in 2005." <u>USA Today.com</u>. 21 Nov.

2006. USA Today. 2 Dec 2008 <http://www.usatoday. com/news/health/2006-11-21-births_x.htm>.

6 "Unchurched Population Nears 100 Million in the U.S." <u>The Barna Update</u>. 19 Mar. 2007 <http://www.barna.org/flex-page.aspx?page=barnaupdate&barnaupdateid=267>.

7 Peirre, Thomas. "Why the Spike in School Shootings?" <u>ABCNews.com</u>. 3 Oct. 2006. ABC News. 2 Dec 2008 <http://www.abcnew.go.com/GMA/story?id=2521025>.

8 "School Associated Violent Deaths and School Shootings." <u>School Security.org</u>. 1 Aug. 2008. National School Safety and Security Services. 2 Dec. 2008 <http:// www.schoolsecurity.org/trends/school_violence.html.

9 Carmona, Richard. "The Obesity Crisis in America." <u>Department of Health and Human Services</u>. 16 July 2003. U.S. Department of Health and Human Services. 2 Dec. 2008 <http://www.surgeongeneral.gov/new/testi-mony/obesity07162003.htm>.

10 DiCaprio, Leonardo. "Polar Bear S. O. S. Campaign Letter." <u>Natural Resources Defense Council</u>. 10 July 2008.

11 "Children of Divorce Parents Are More Likely to Themselves Divorce." <u>The Journal of Young Investigators</u>. 13 (27 July 2005). Journal of Young Investigators Inc. 2 Dec. 2008 <http://www.jyi.org/news/nb.php?id=352>.

12 Bounds, Edward. <u>Purpose in Prayer</u>. New Kensington: Whitaker House, 1997.

13 Cymbala, Jim and Dean Merril. <u>Fresh Wind, Fresh Fire:</u> <u>What Happens When God's Spirit Invades the Hearts of</u> <u>His People</u>. Grand Rapids: Zondervan, 1997.

14 Black, Robert, Jennifer Bryce, and Saul Morris. "Where and Why are 10 Million Children Dying Every Year?" <u>The Lancet</u> 361 (2003): 2226-2234.

15 See above citation for Carmona, Richard.

16 Henry, Matthew. <u>Matthew Henry's Concise Commentary</u> <u>on the Whole Bible</u>. Nashville: Thomas Nelson, 1997.

Breinigsville, PA USA
28 January 2010
231554BV00001B/2/P